Behind The Lines
Thoughts And Feelings In Black, White And Gray
By
South Dakota Inmates

Copyright © 2018 Family Connection

All rights reserved. No part of this book may be reproduced or transmitted in any form or by any means without written permission of the publisher, authors, editor and copyright holder. The copyright is non-transferable without the written permission of the authors and editor.

ISBN:1729626335
ISBN-13:978-1729626337

DEDICATION

Dedicated to those commited to prison reform and reducing the number of inmate who return to prison after being released.

Dedicated to those engaged in help inmates become more useful and full members of society while finding purpose and fulfillment in their lives.

Dedicated to members of the pubic who support efforts to reduce the need for prisons in our society.

Edited by
Lawrence Diggs
Volunteer South Dakota Department of Corrections

Proceeds from the sale of this book go to Family Connection. Family Connection provides Hospitality Houses that provide shelter for families traveling to Sioux Falls to visit an incarcerated loved one. This service allows families with limited incomes to continue the healing process with an incarcerated family member.

Children's Connection, a United Way Agency, works with the Sioux Falls School District to provide group counseling services to children with an incarcerated family member. Children with a parent in prison are more likely to be incarcerated themselves. Family Connections, through the Children's Connection program, is working to break this cycle.

Your support is greatly appreciated.

Artist Roster

Alvin Plastow
Chris Hartford
Christopher Carroll-Tutino
Dean Cochrun
Dennis Evenson
Devin Galloway
Edward Flad
Ernest Fisher
James Shaw
Jamie Wright
Jon Jolley
Joseph Golliher-Weyer
Michael Sedlmeier
Paul Wentzel
Richard Traversie
Shane Archer
Shane Blake
Tyson Hayes

Alvin Plastow

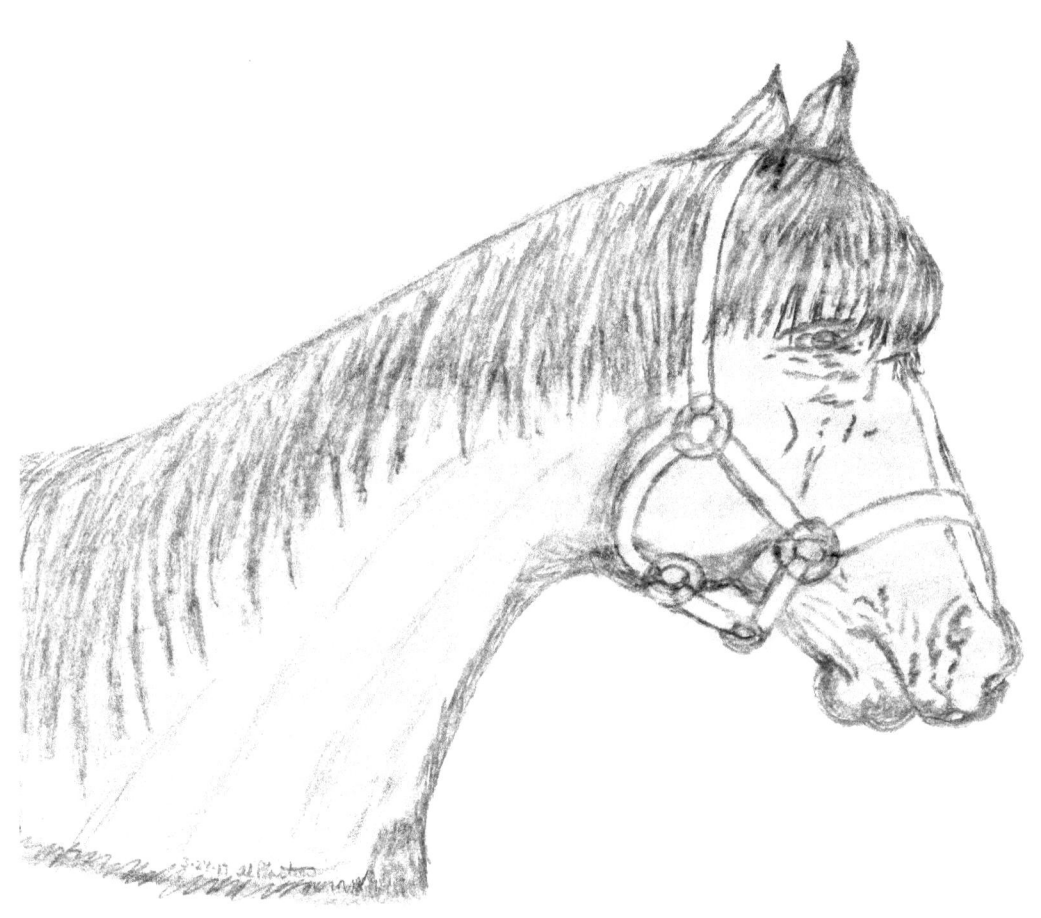

Alvin Plastow

ROOSTER

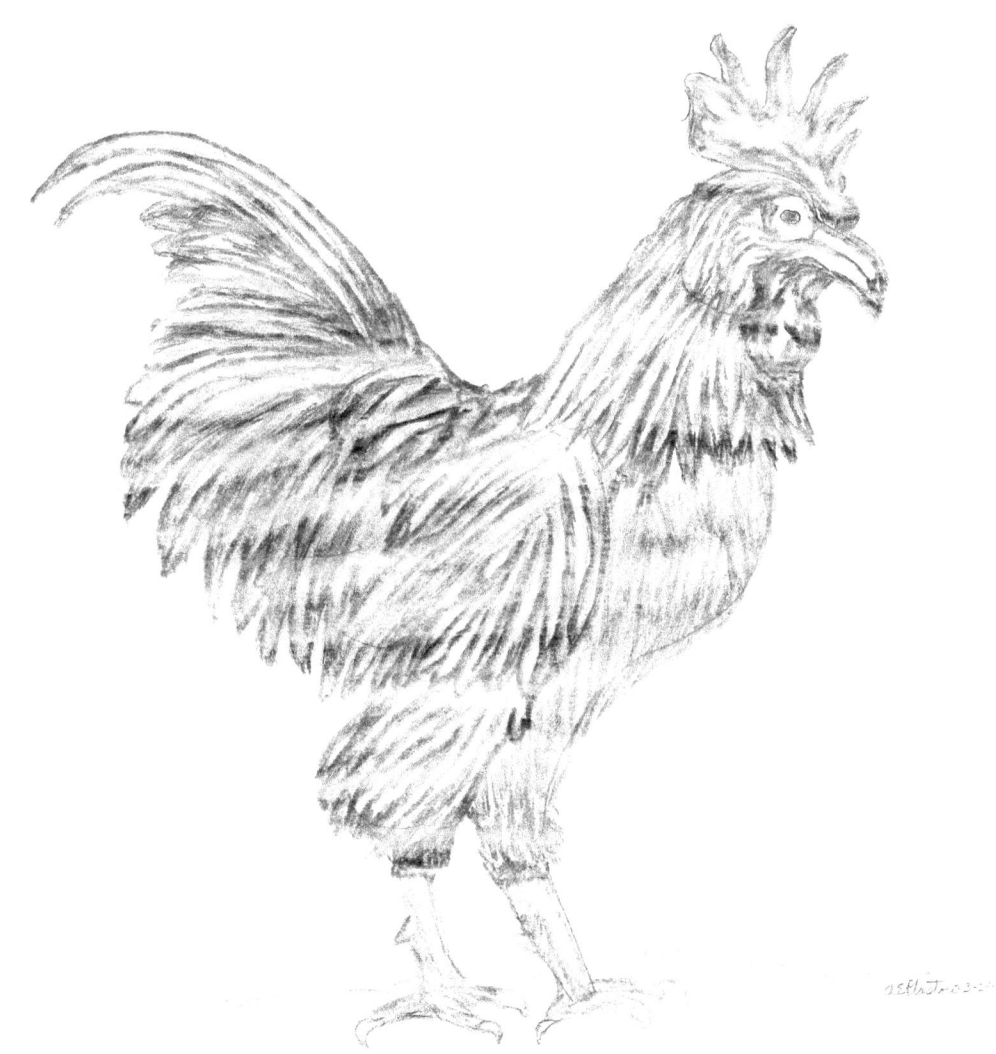

Chris Hartford

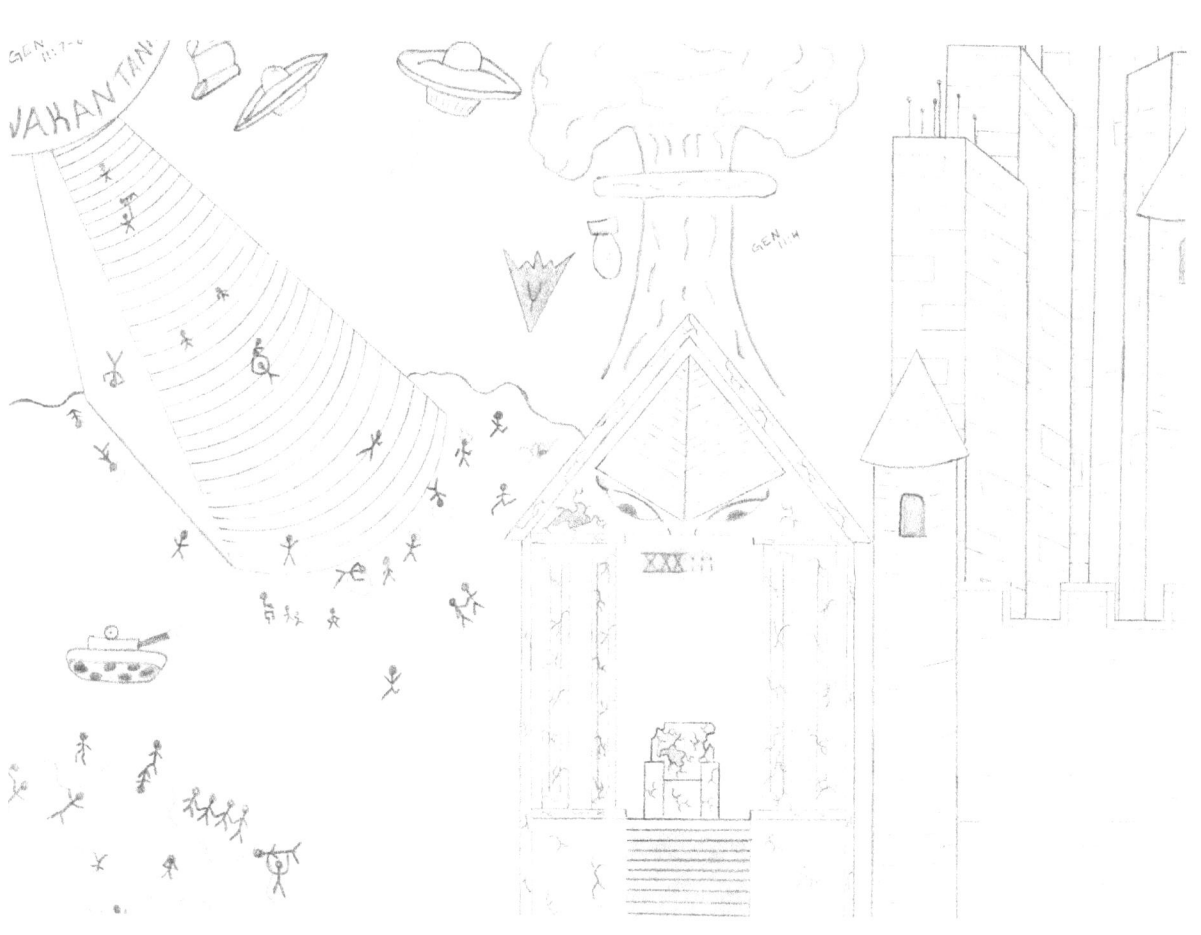

Chris Hartford

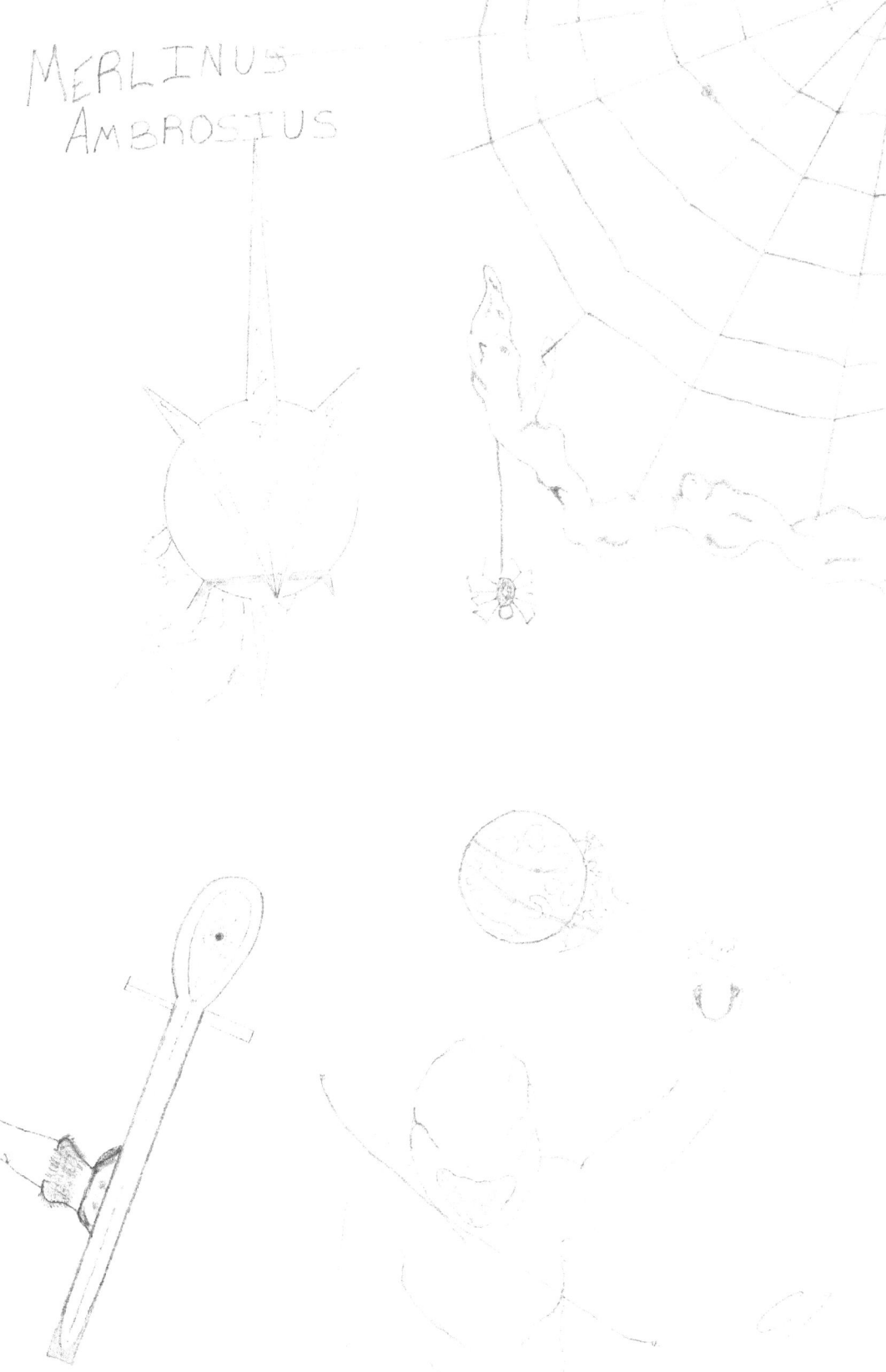

Chris Hartford

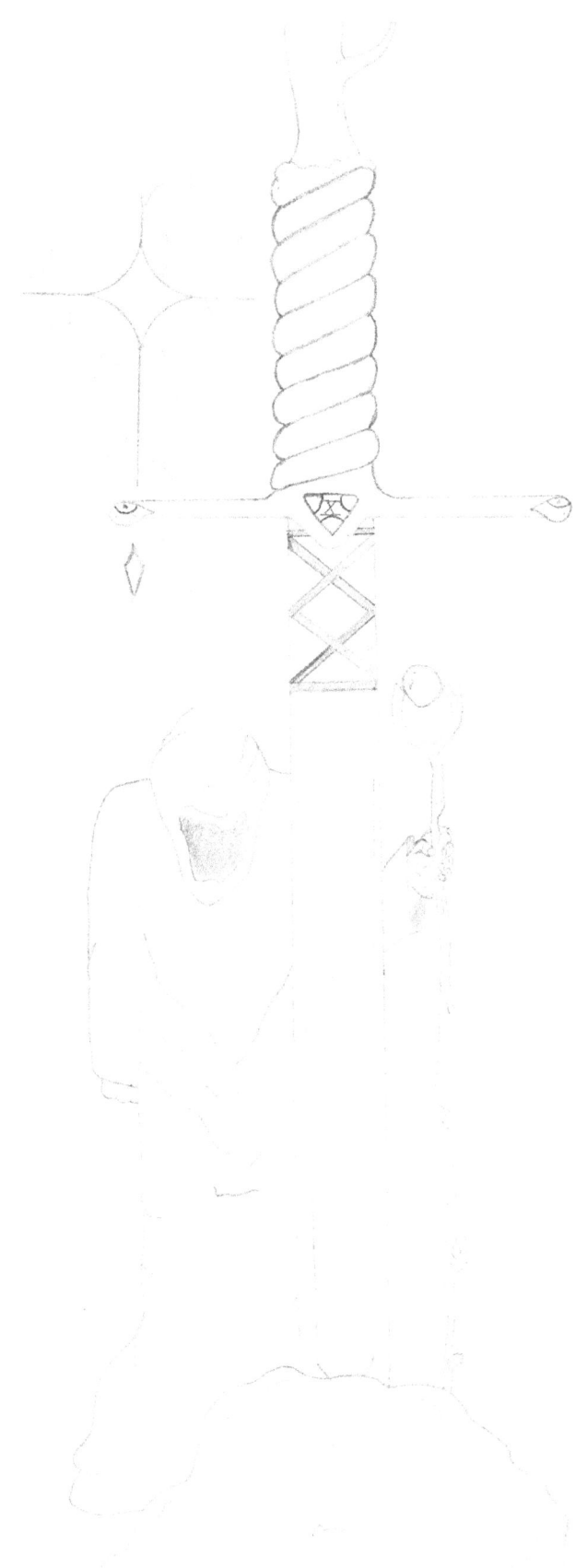

Chris Hartford

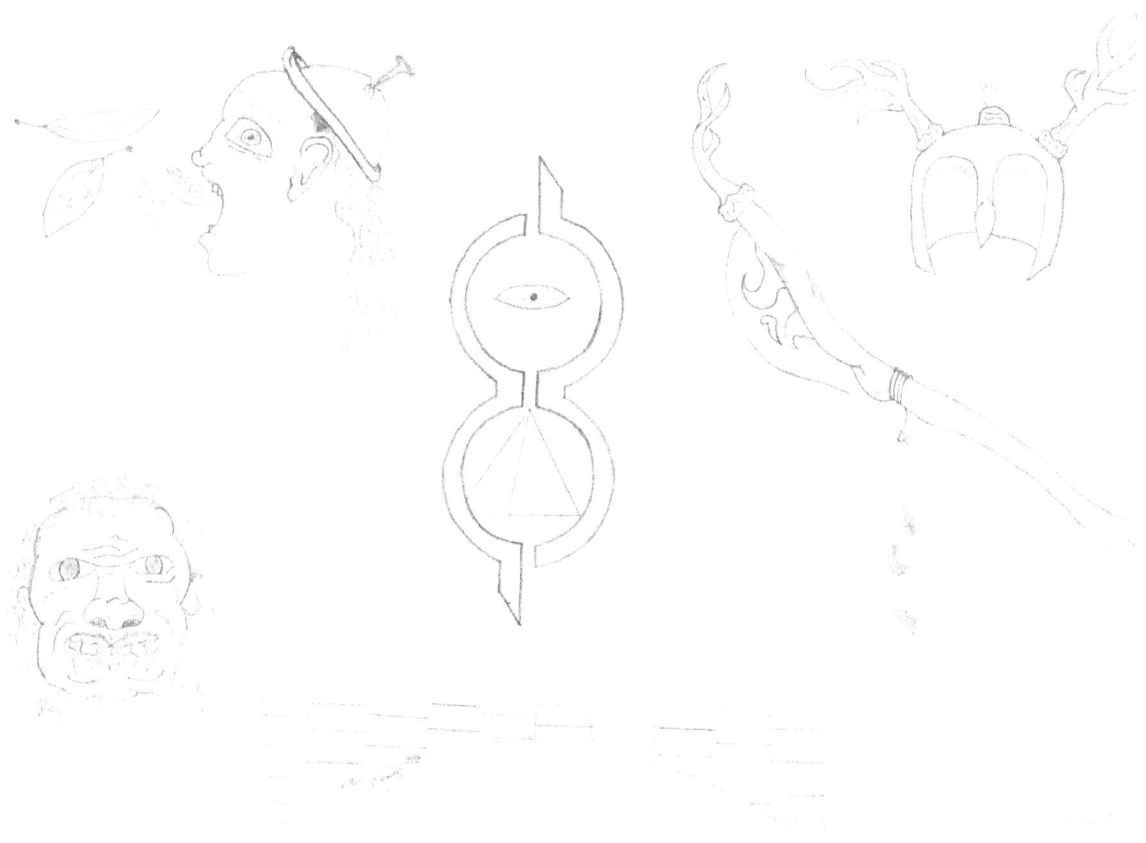

Christopher Carroll-Tutino

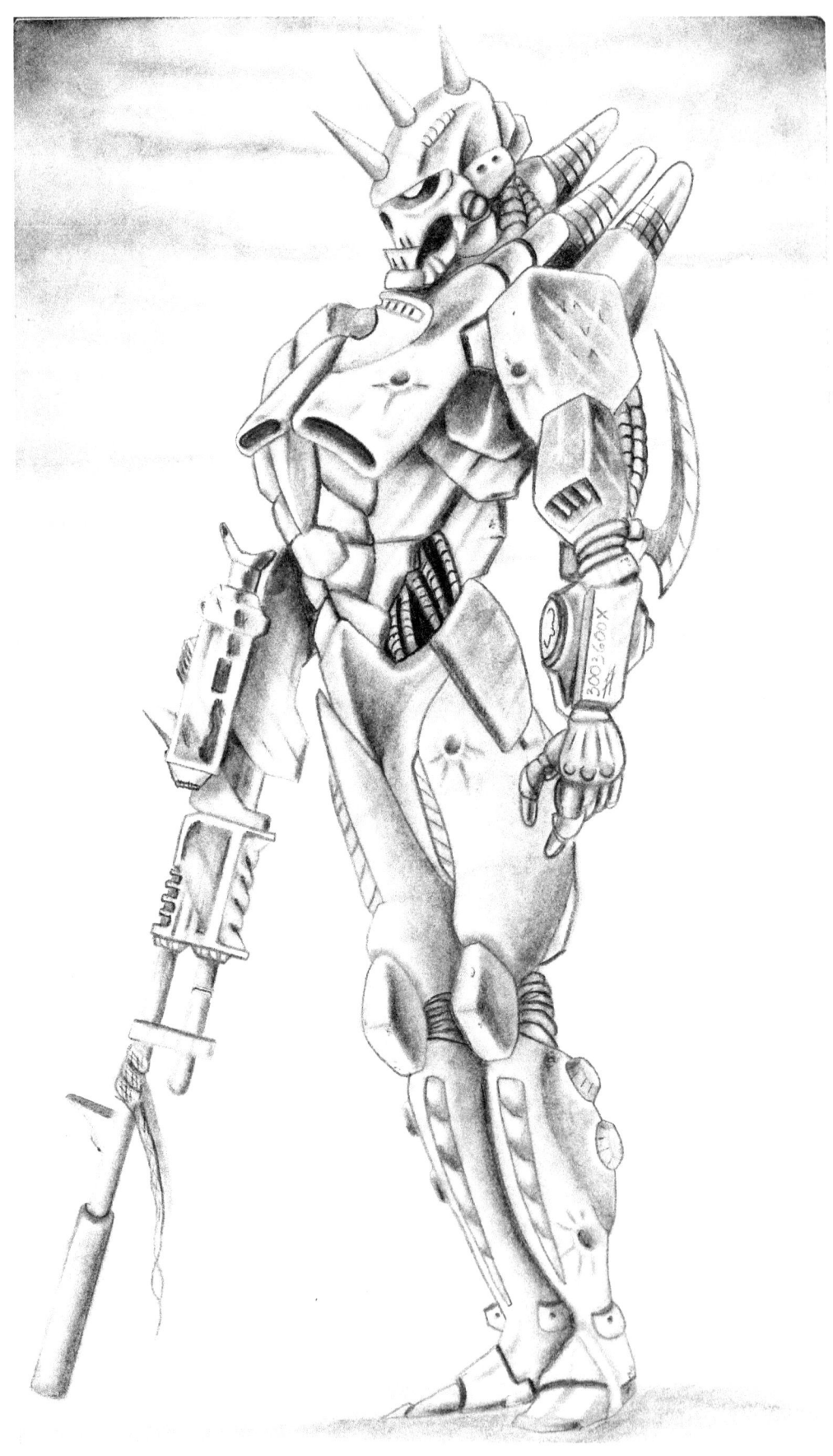

Christopher Carroll-Tutino

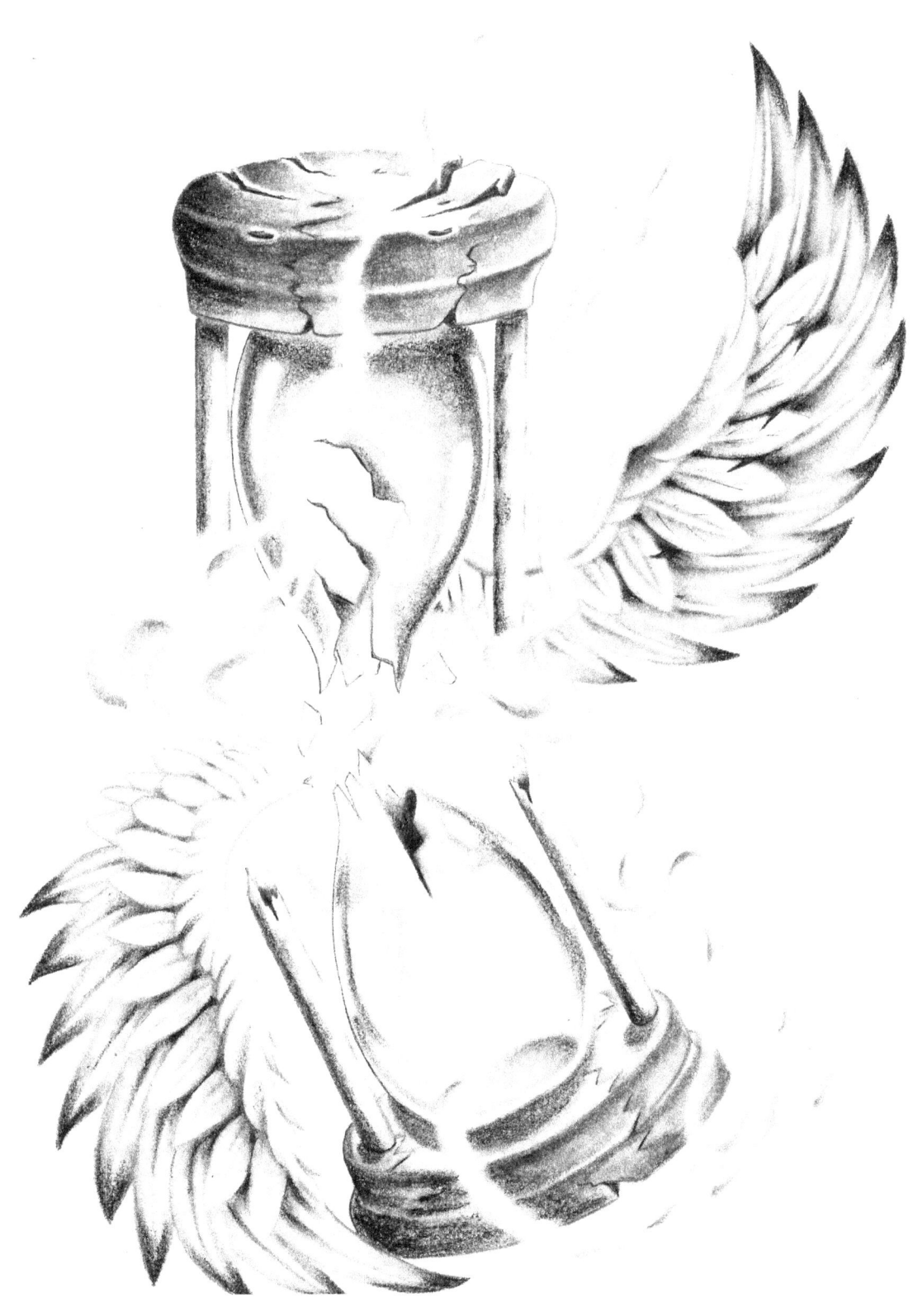

Christopher Carroll-Tutino

Christopher Carroll-Tutino

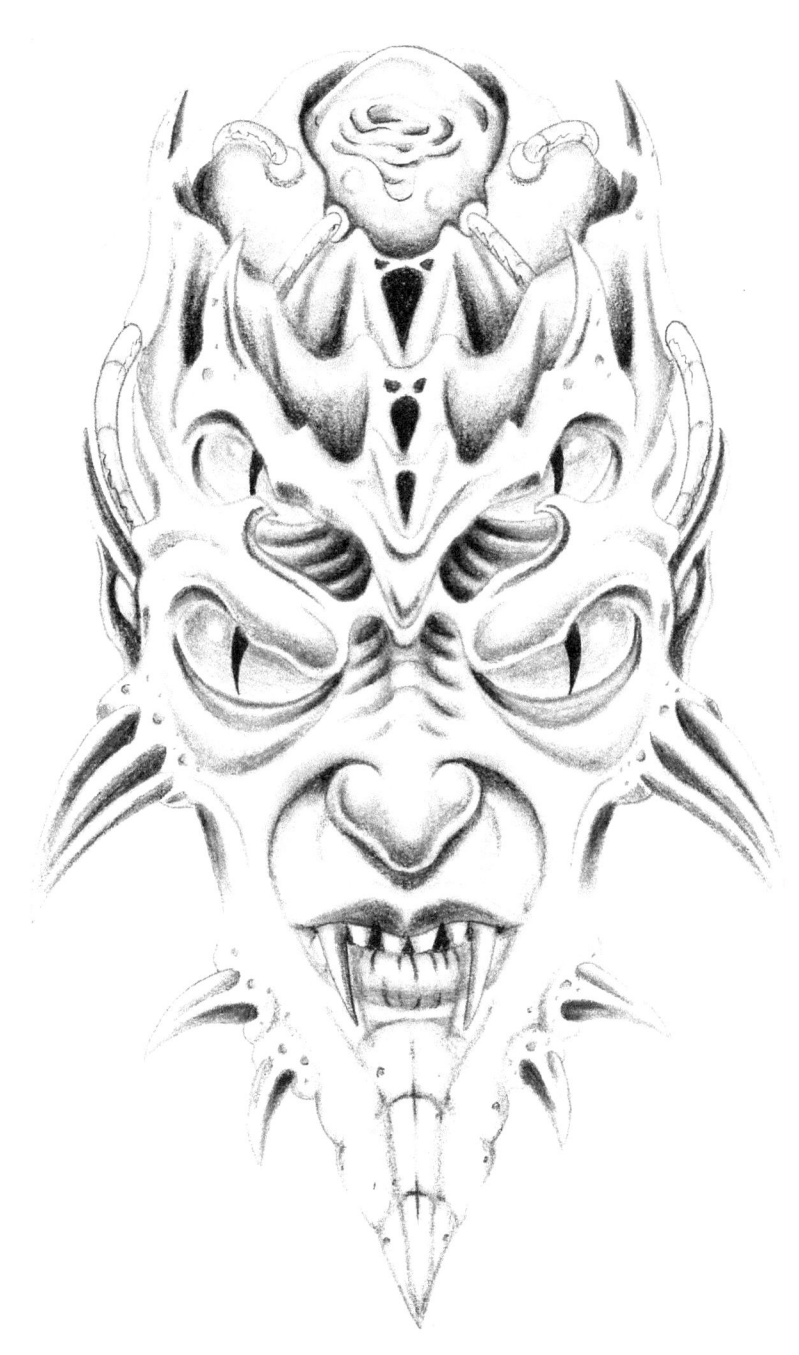

Christopher Carroll-Tutino

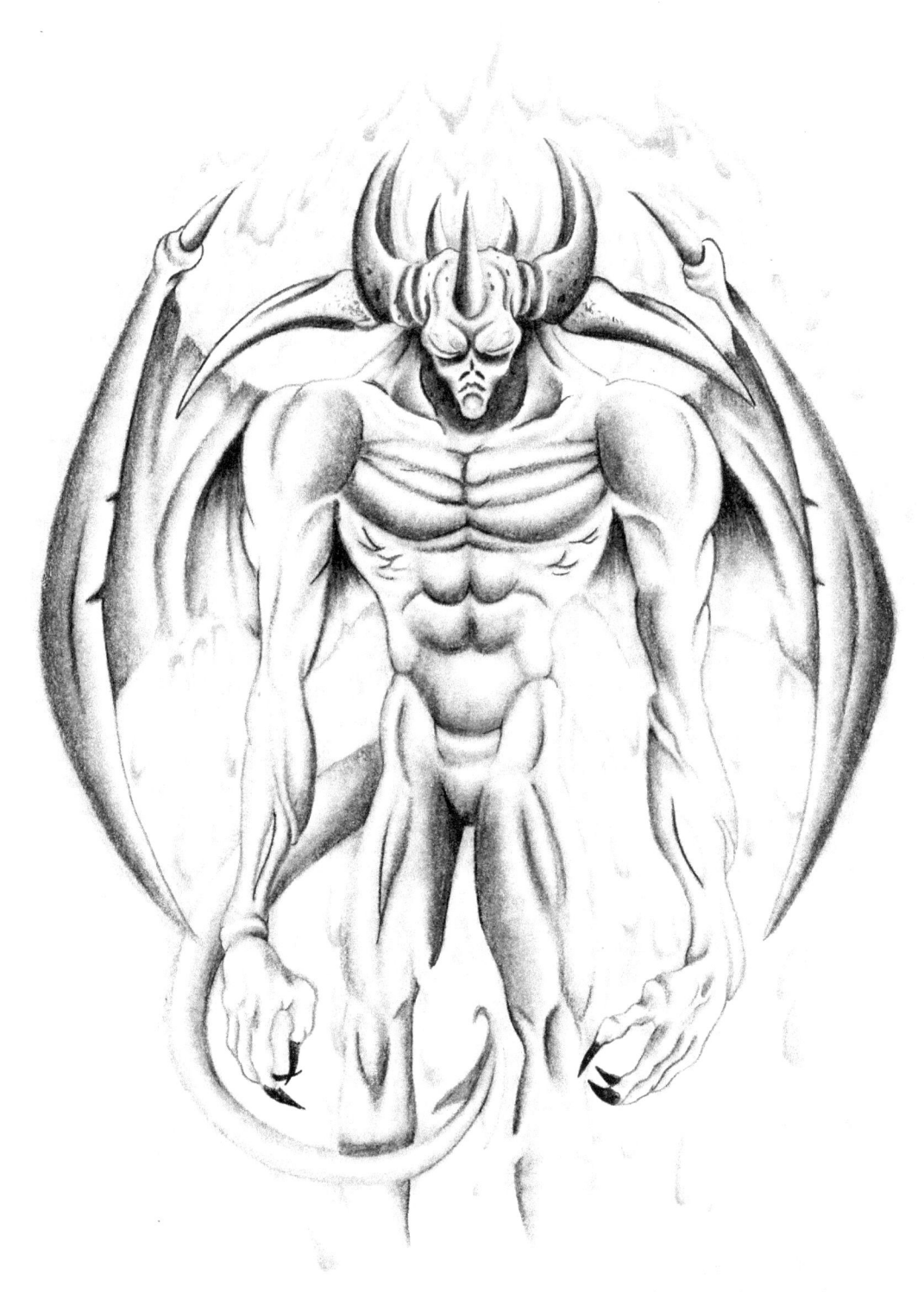

Christopher Carroll-Tutino

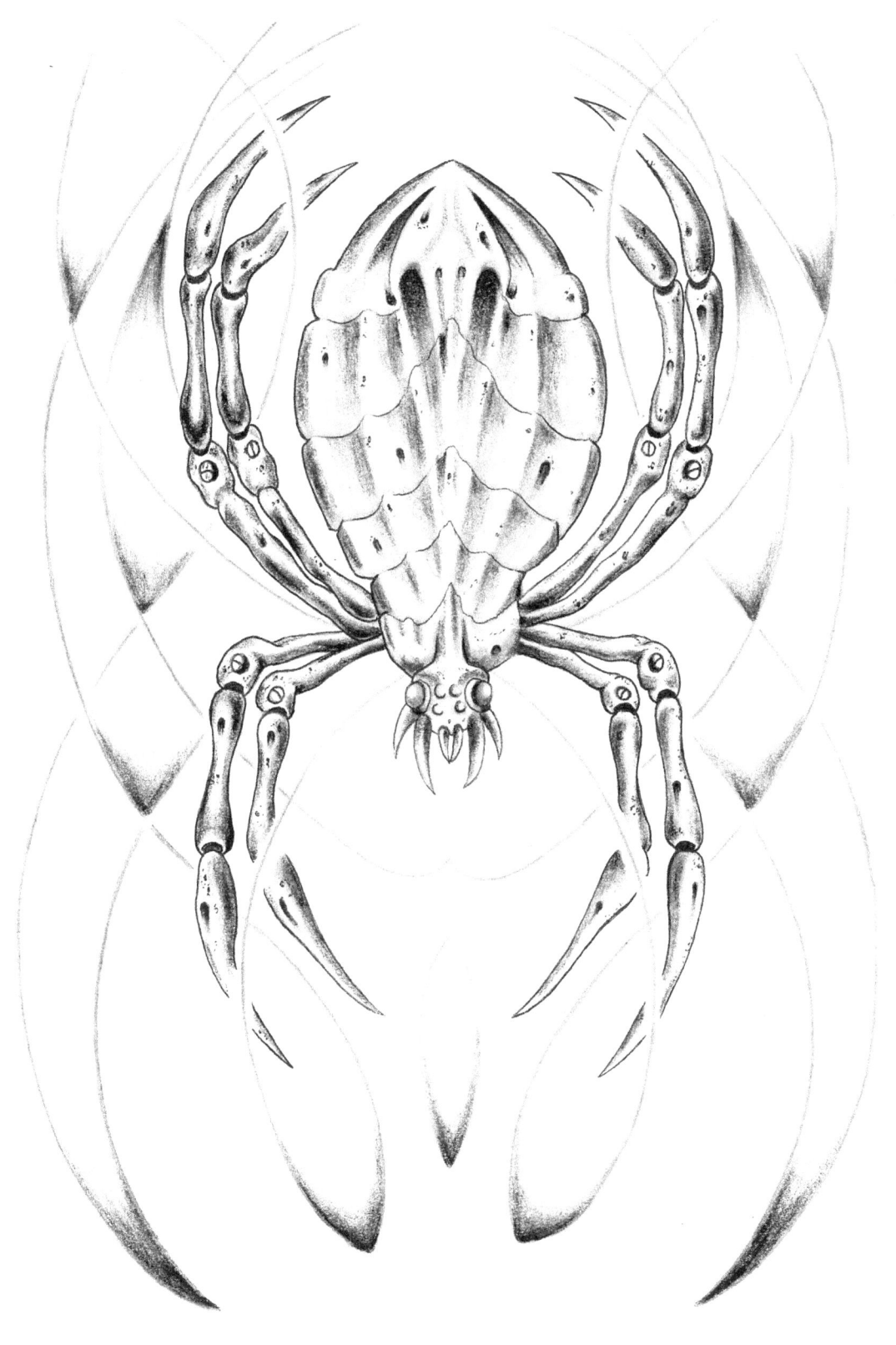

Christopher Carroll-Tutino

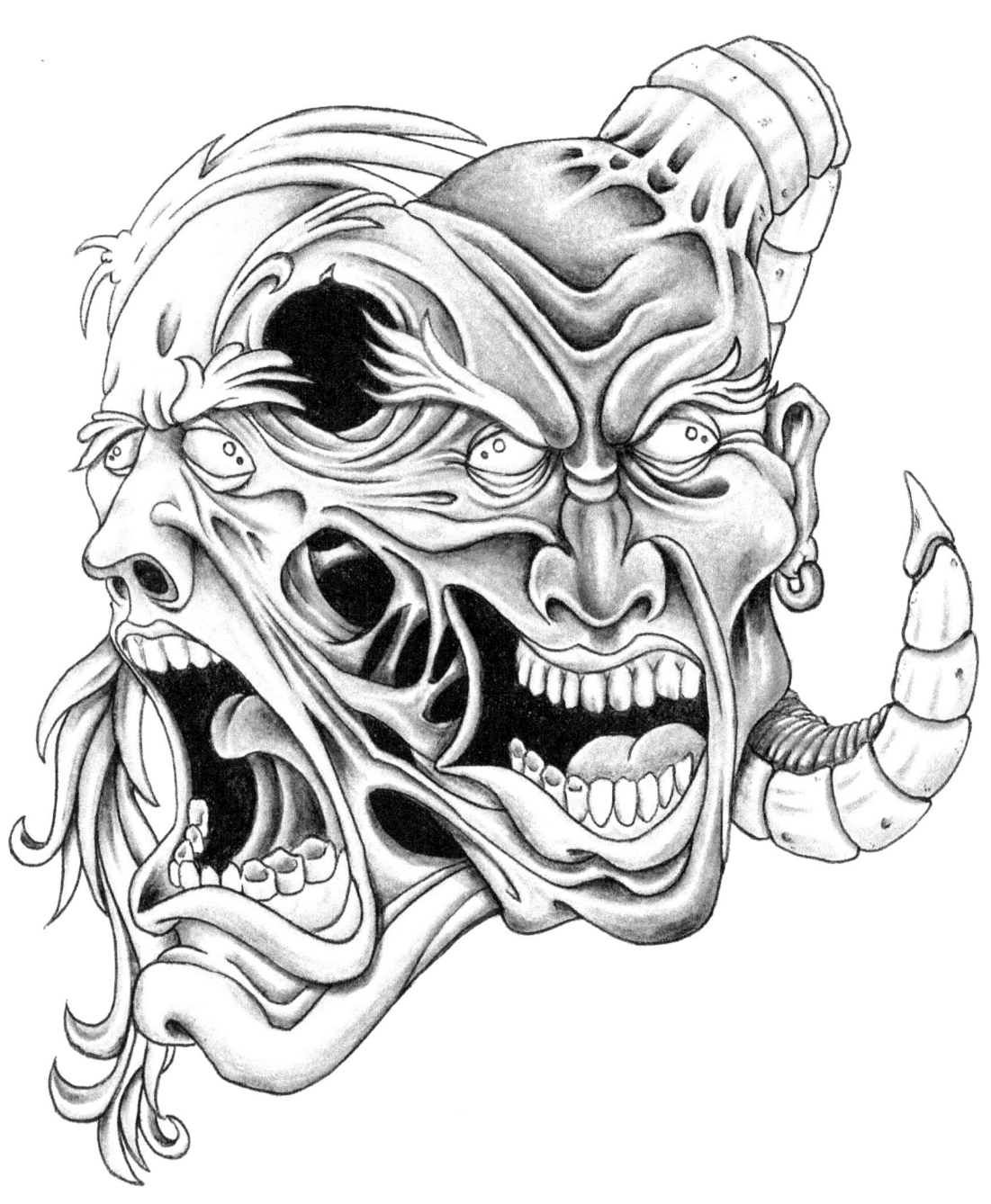

Christopher Carroll-Tutino

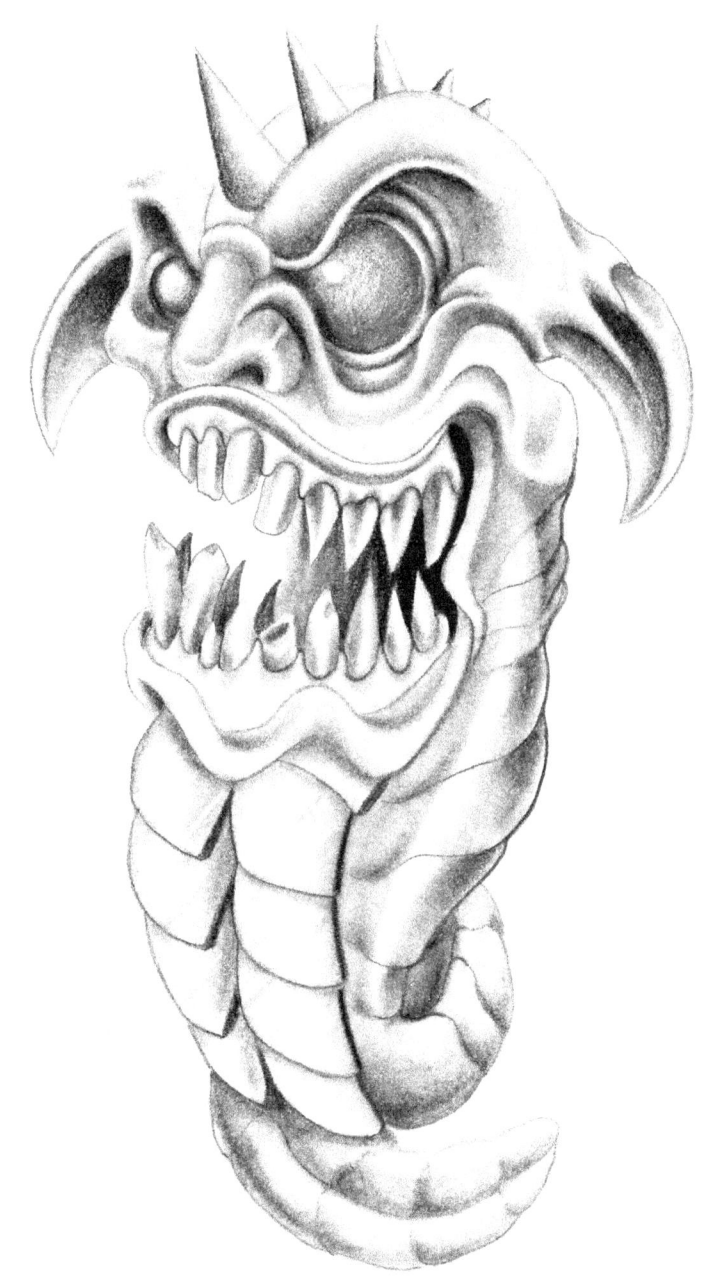

Christopher Carroll-Tutino

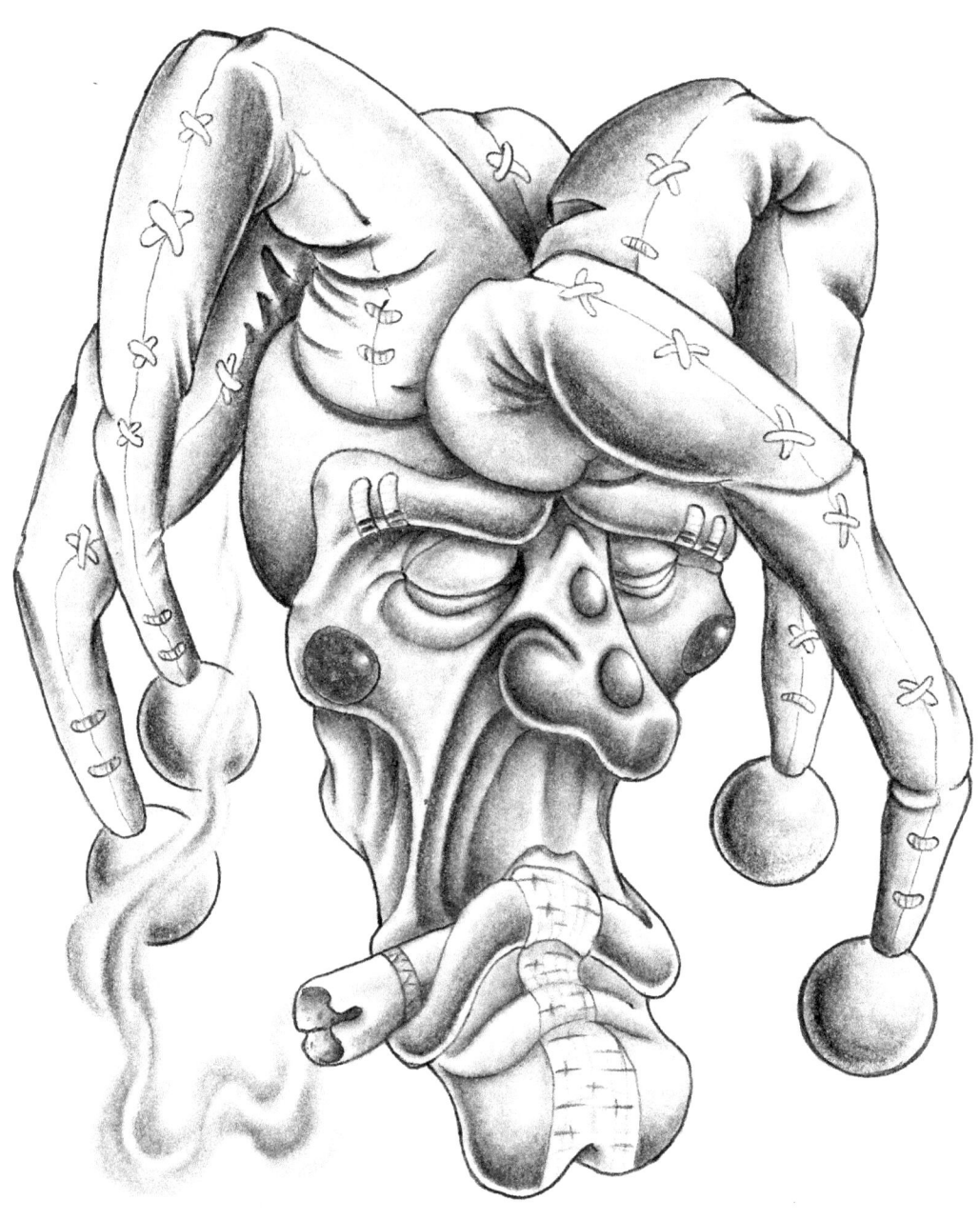

Christopher Carroll-Tutino

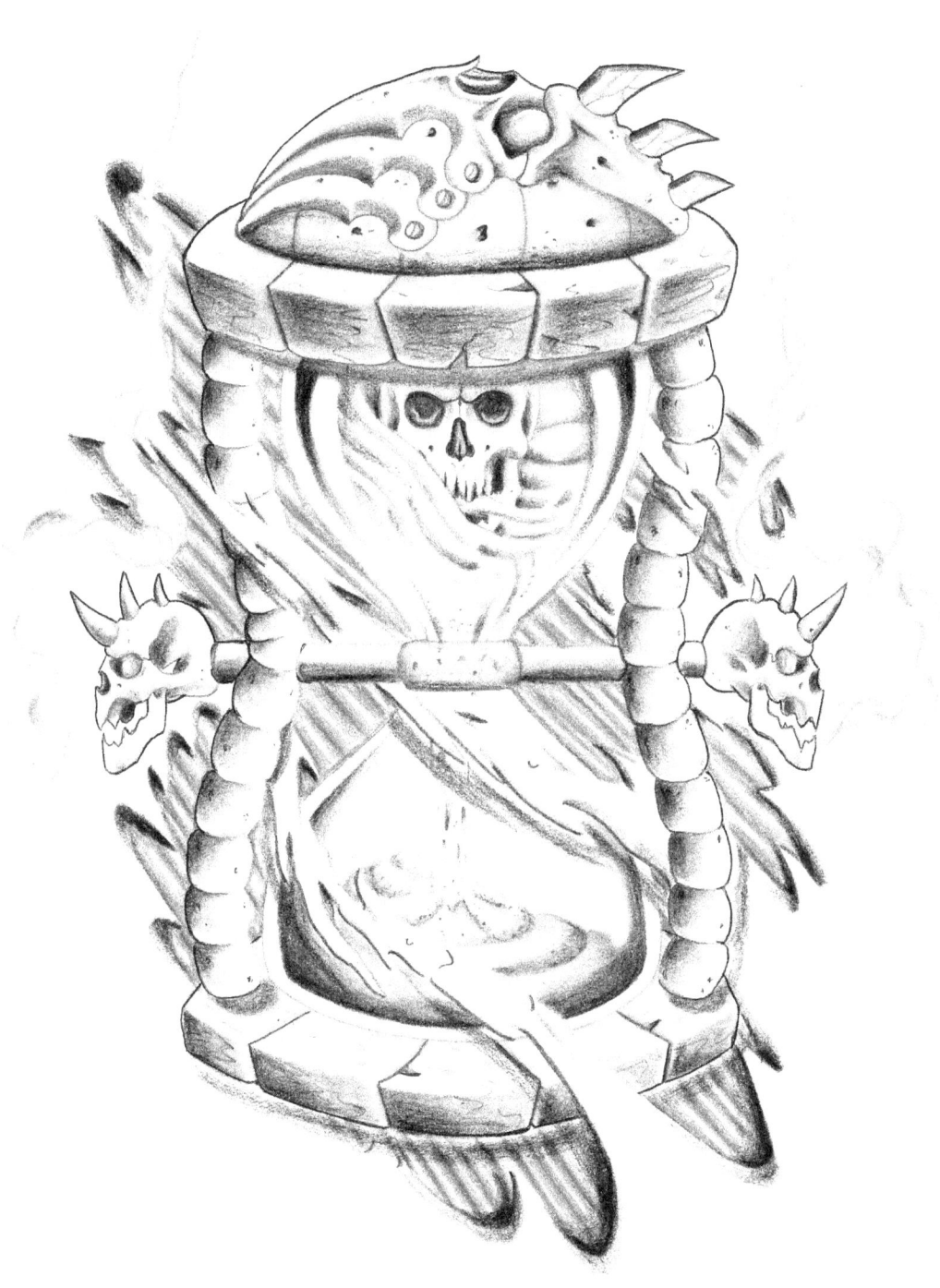

Christopher Carroll-Tutino

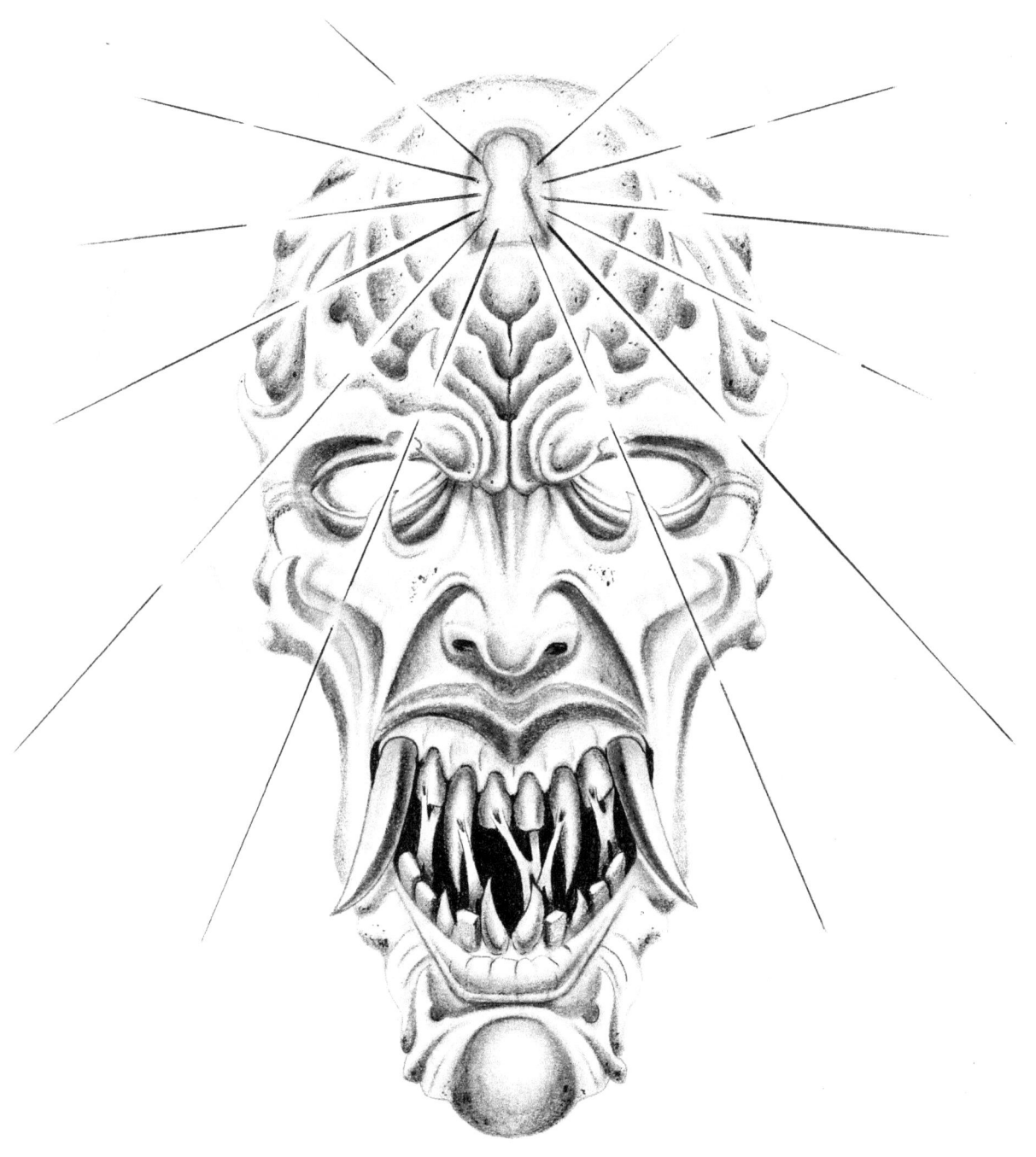

Christopher Carroll-Tutino

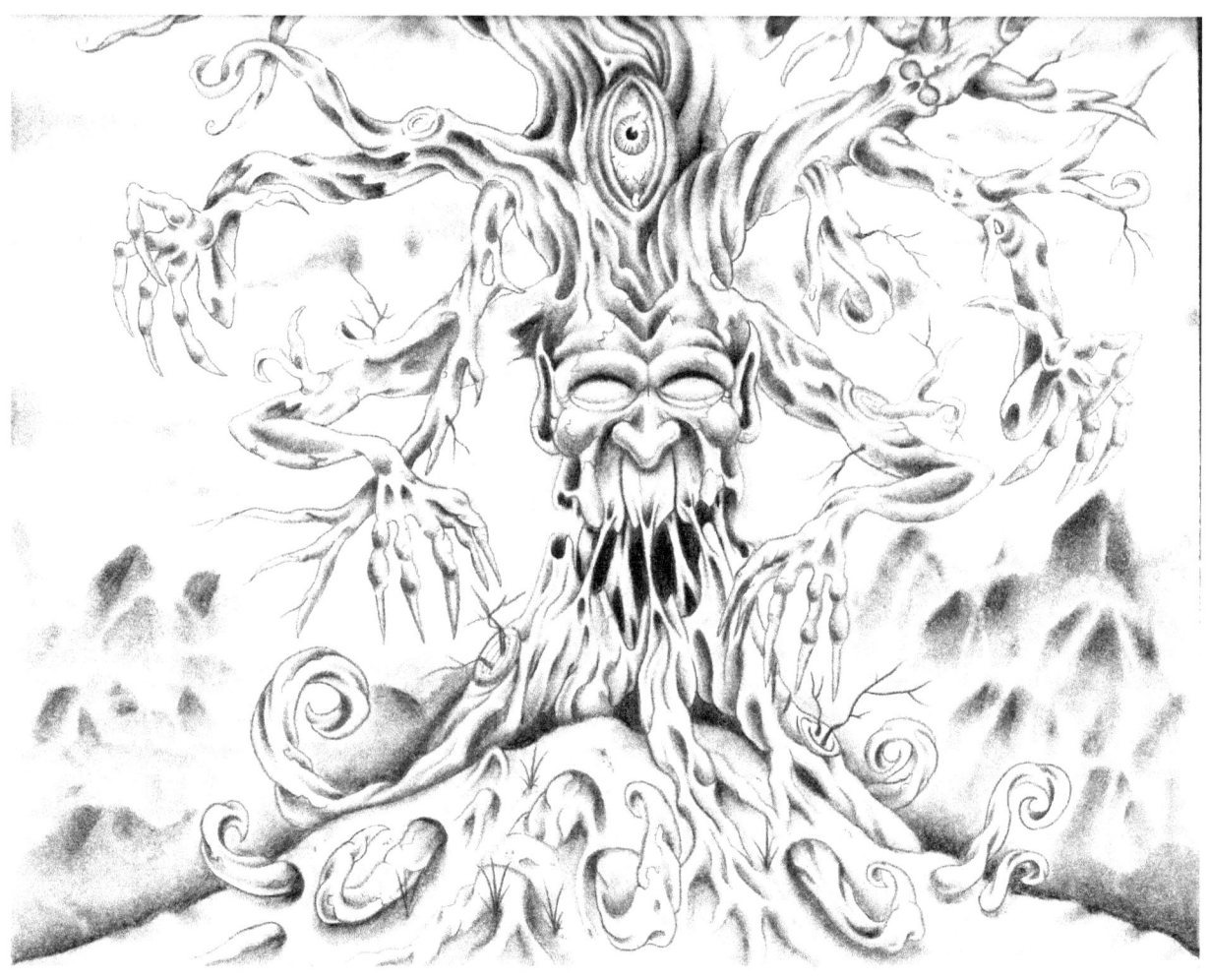

Christopher Carroll-Tutino

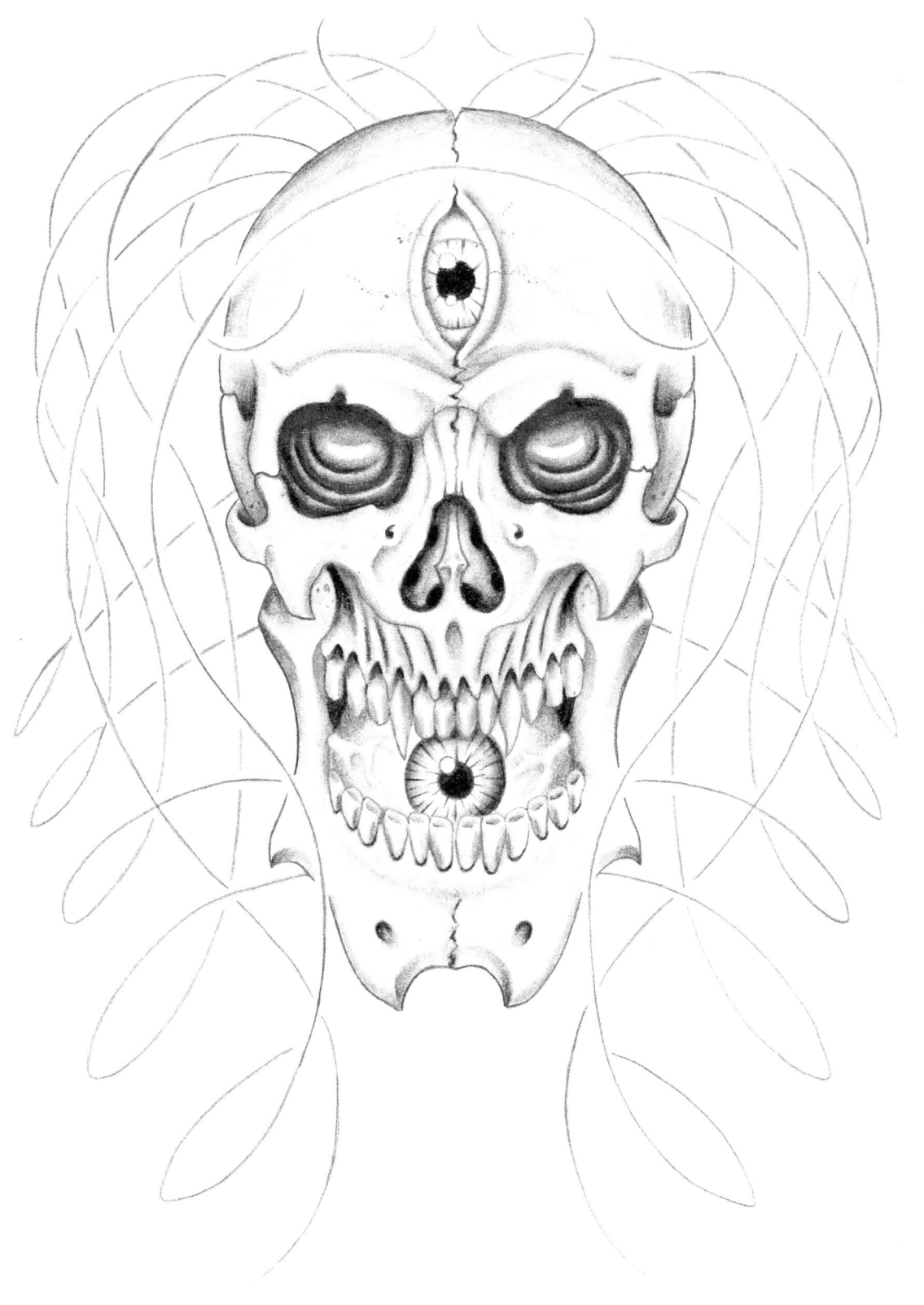

Dean Cochrun

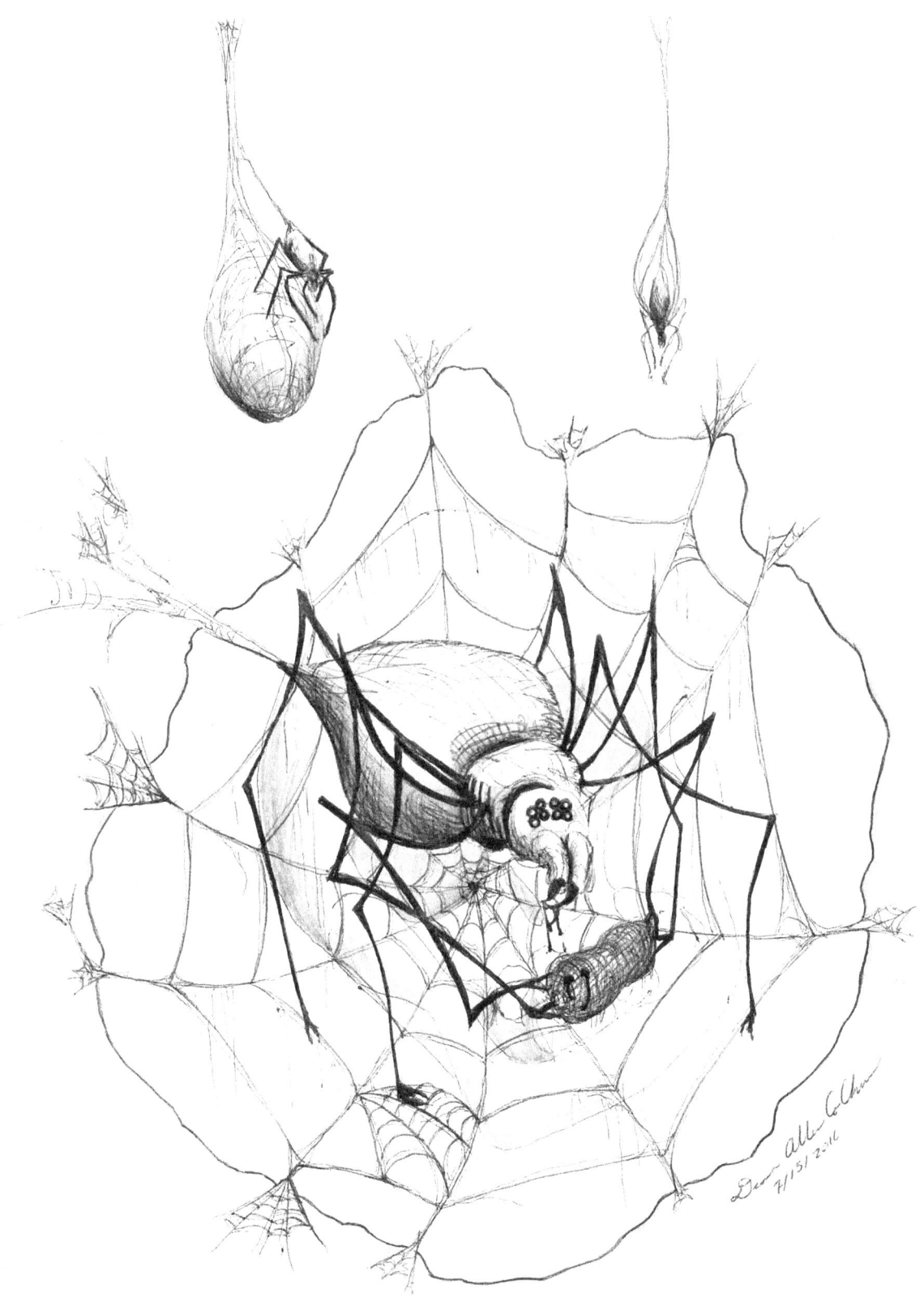

Dennis Evenson

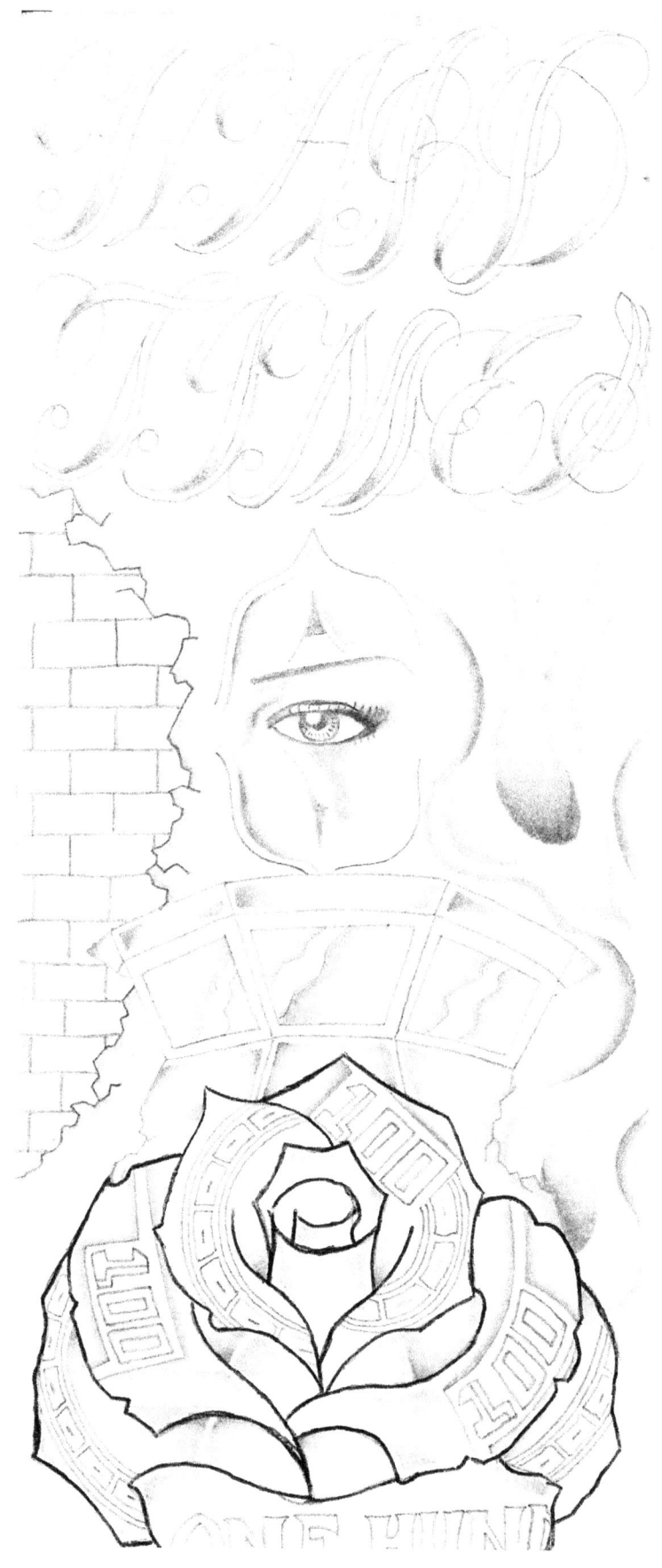

Dennis Evenson

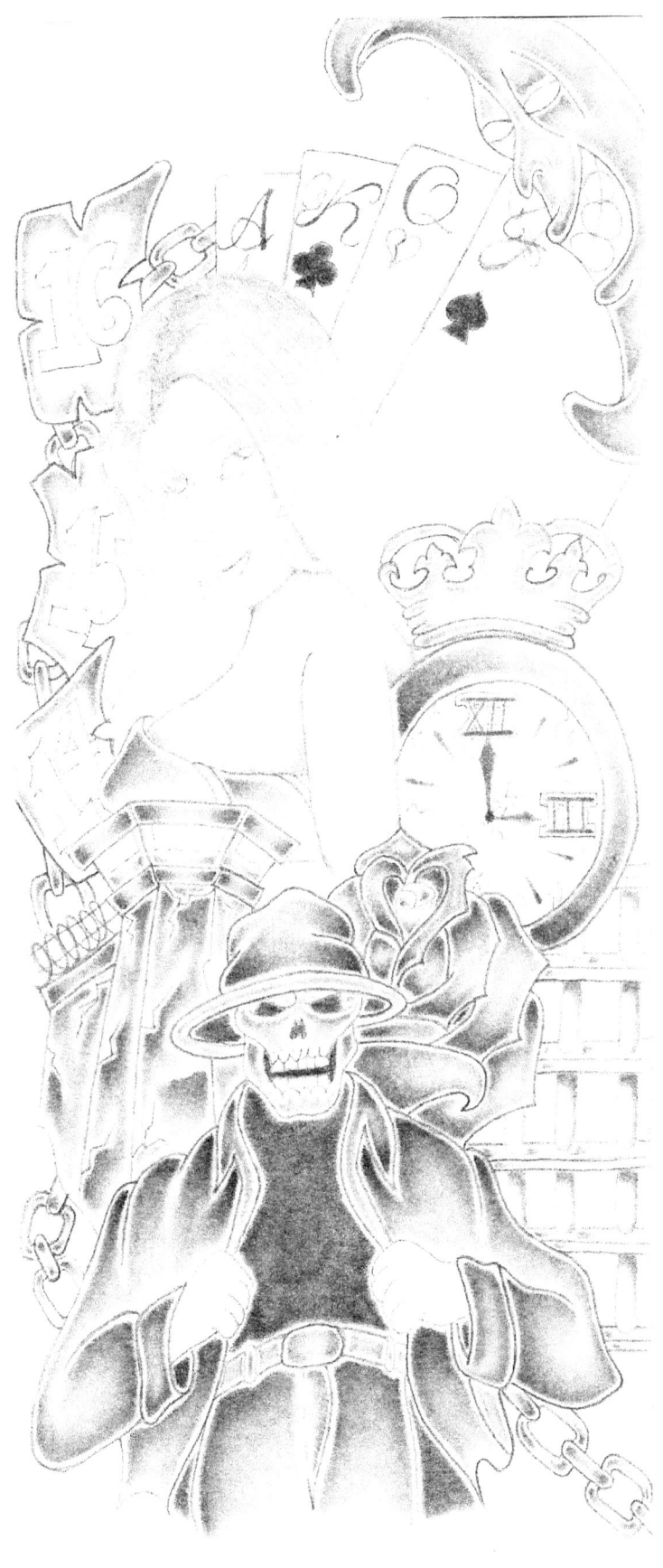

Devin Galloway

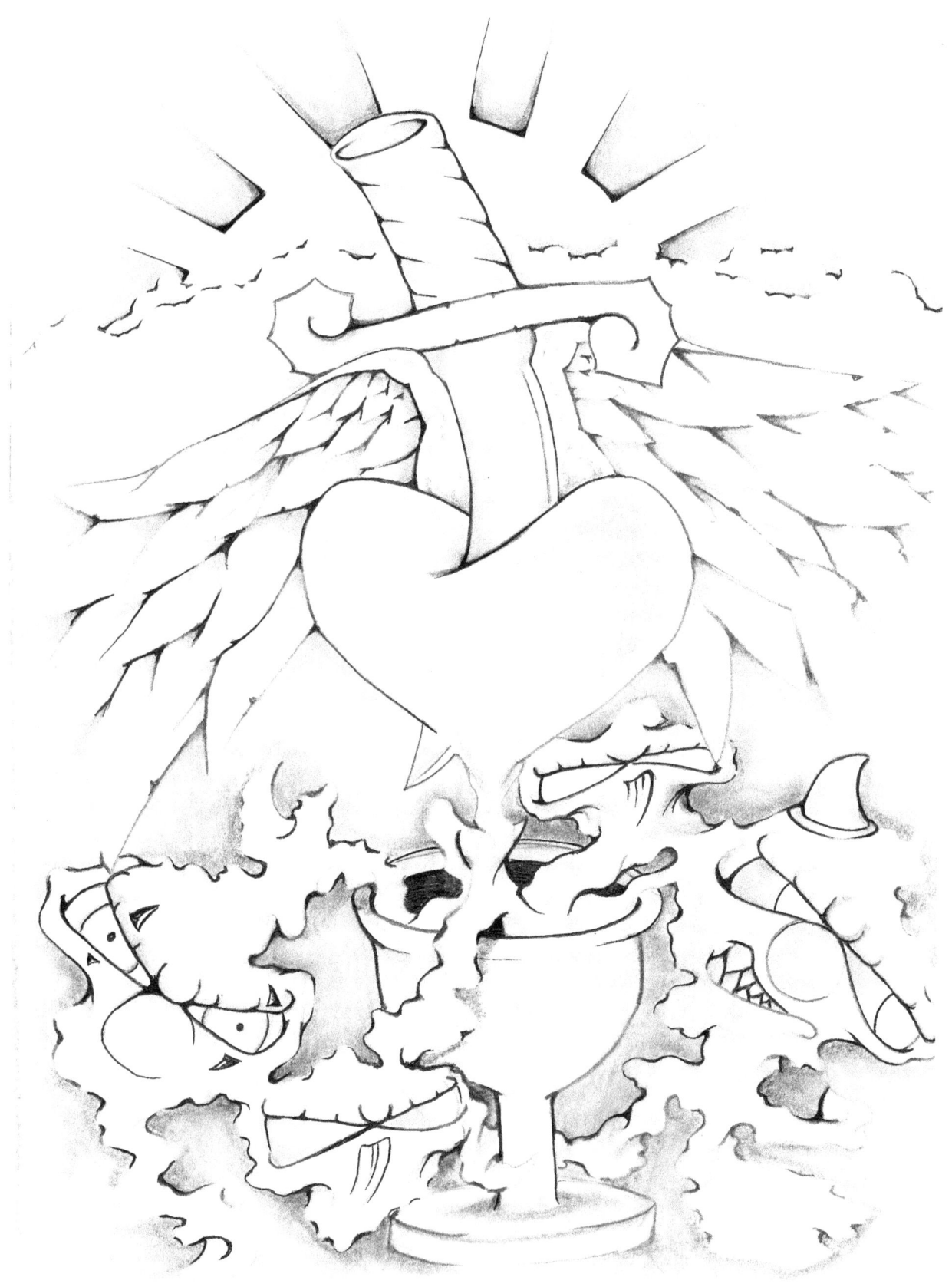

Devin Galloway

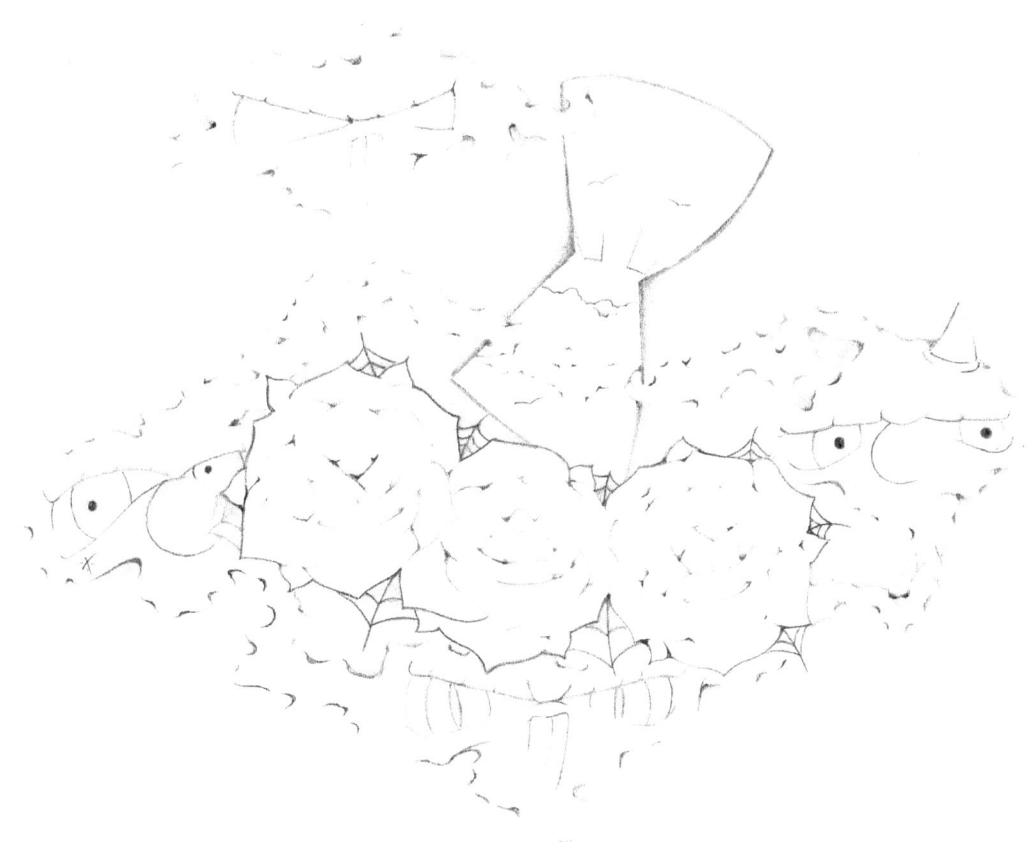

Edward Flad

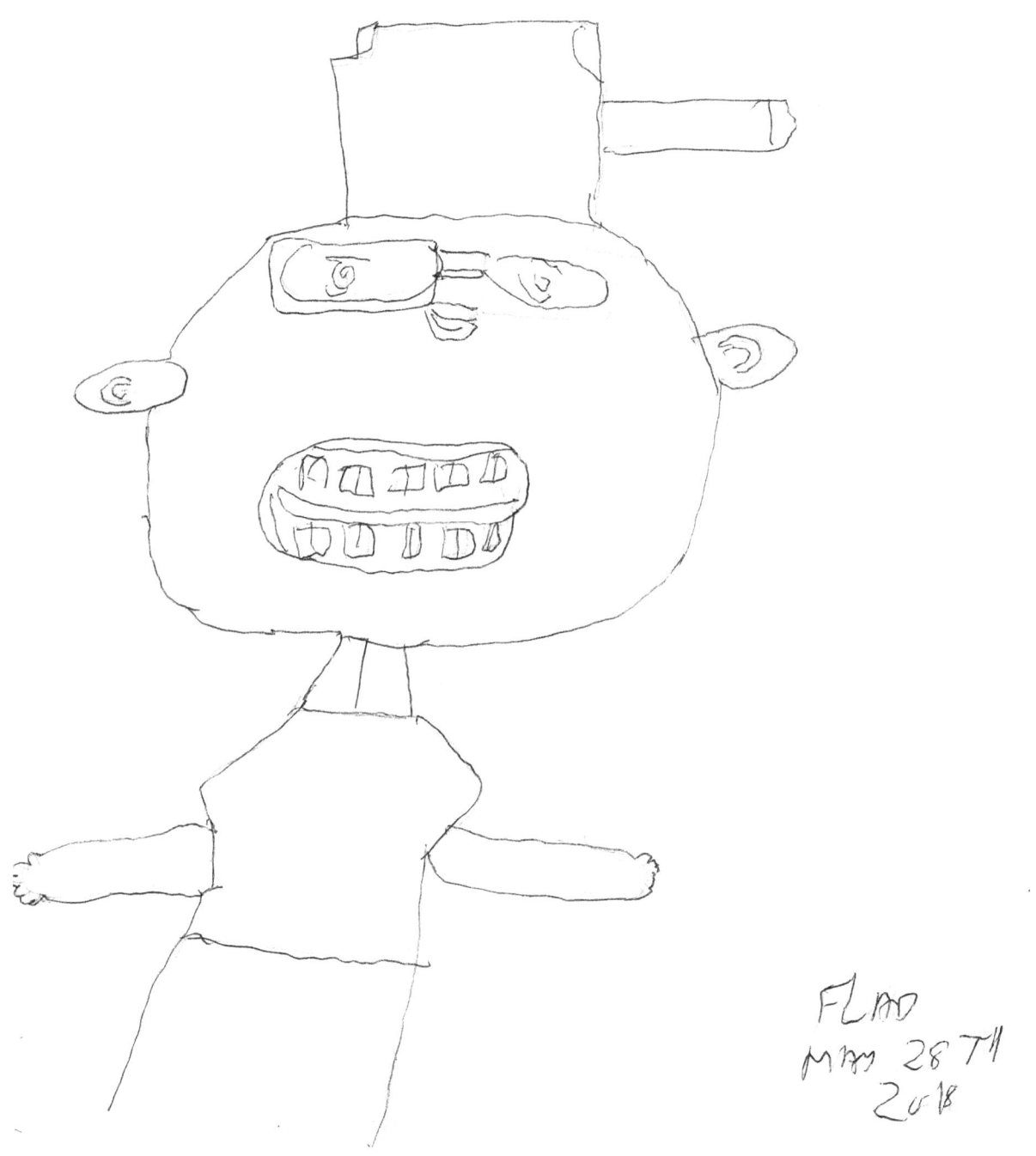

Edward Flad

Edward Flad

Ernest Fisher

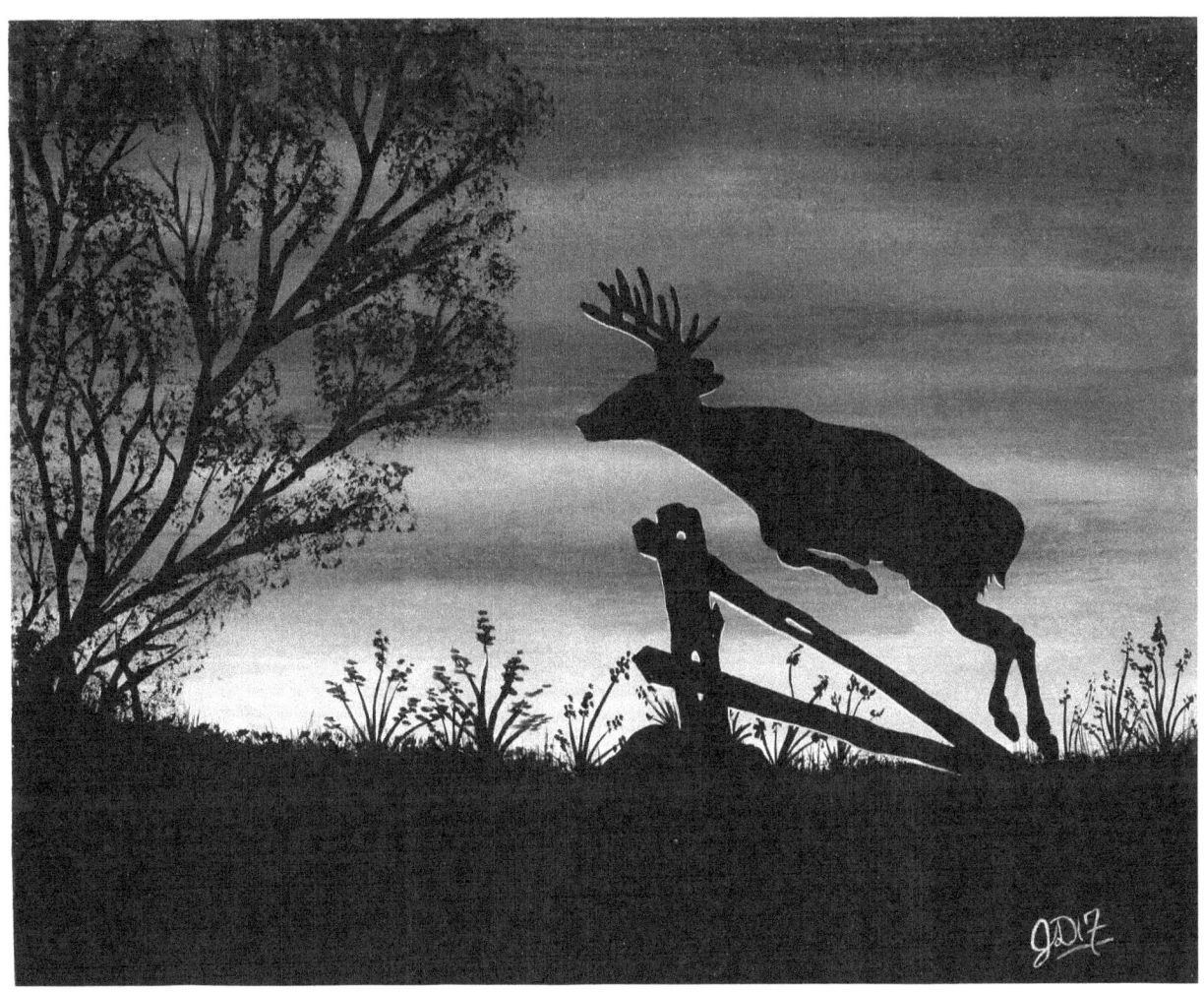

Ernest Fisher

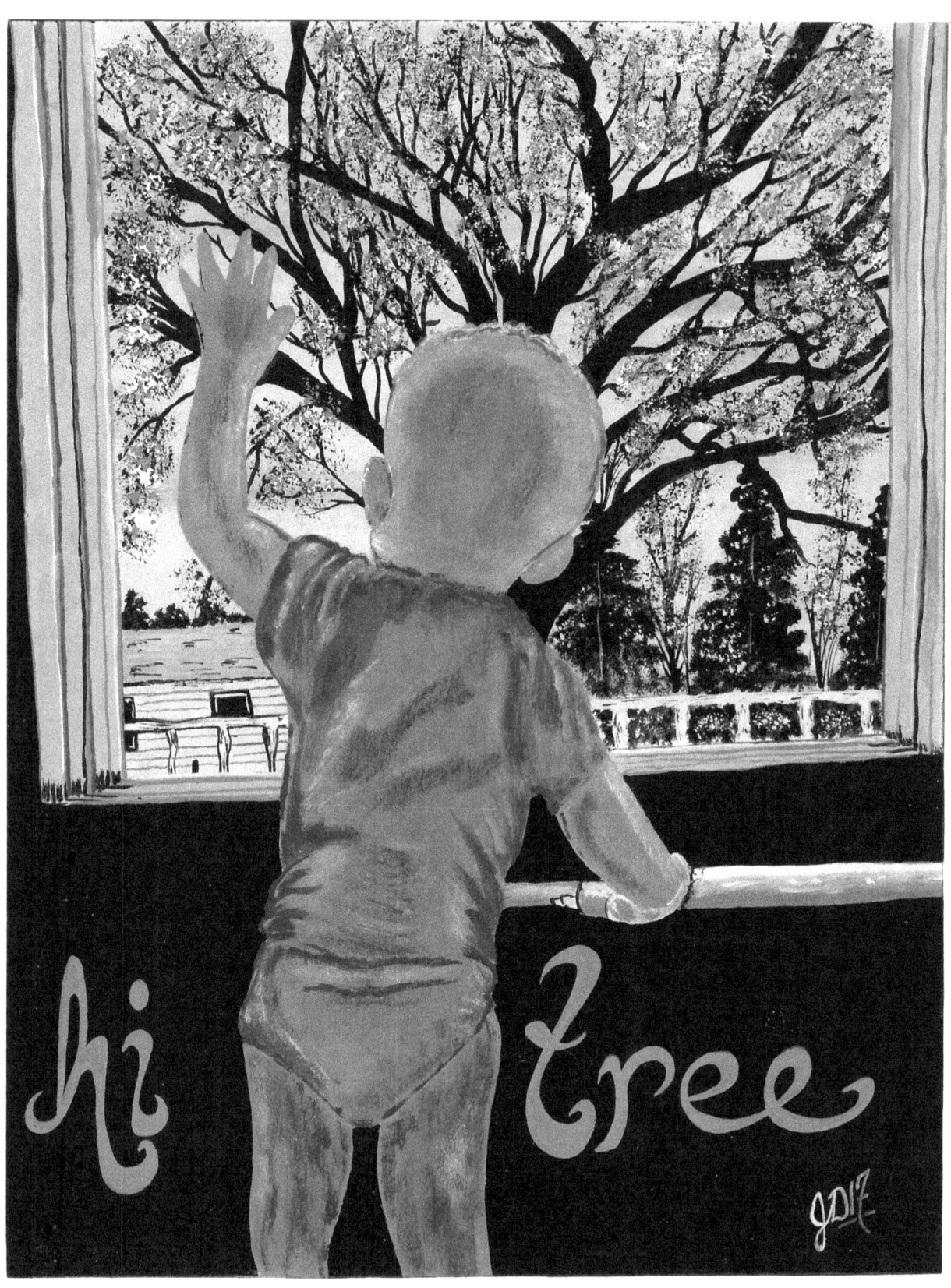

Ernest Fisher

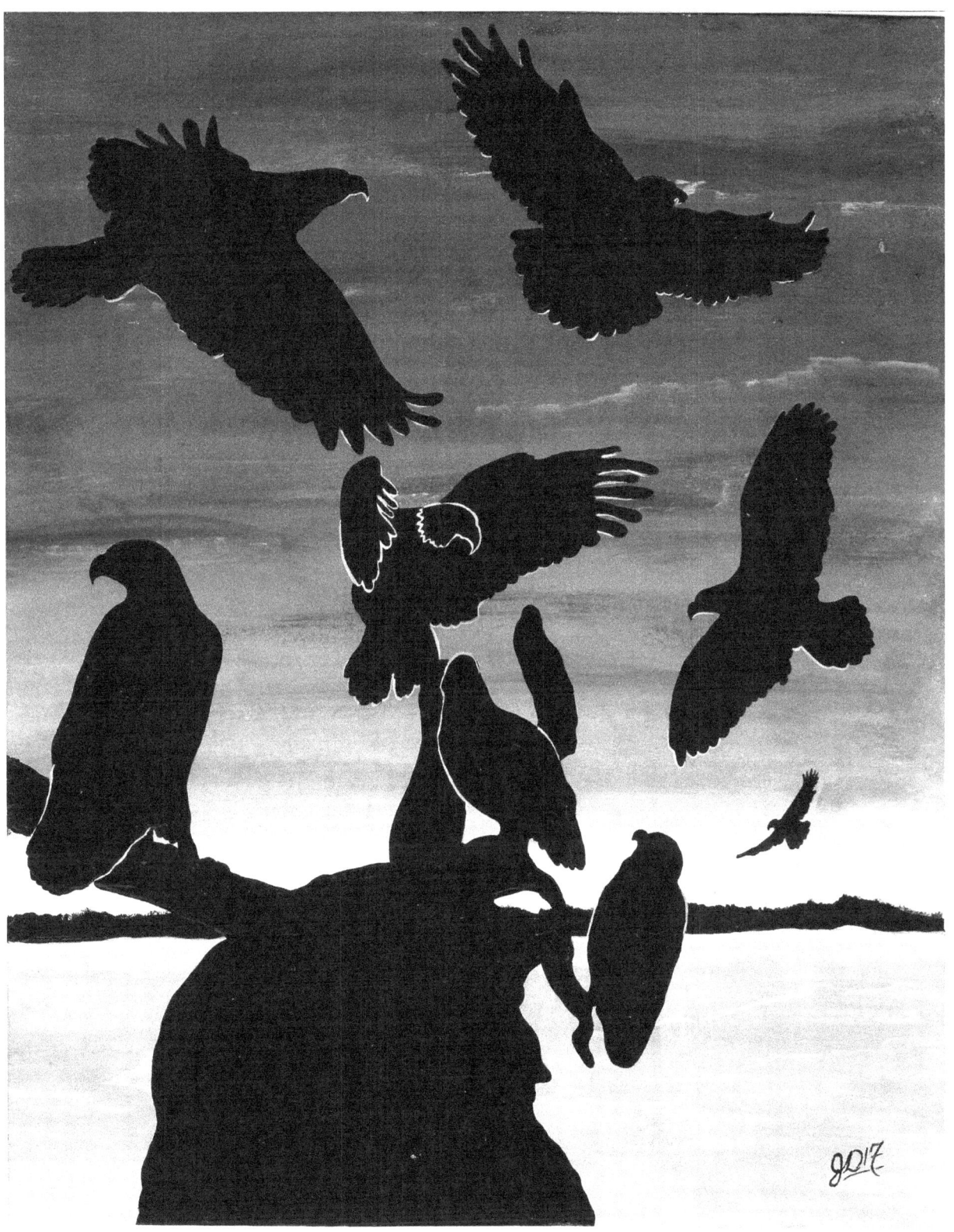

James Shaw

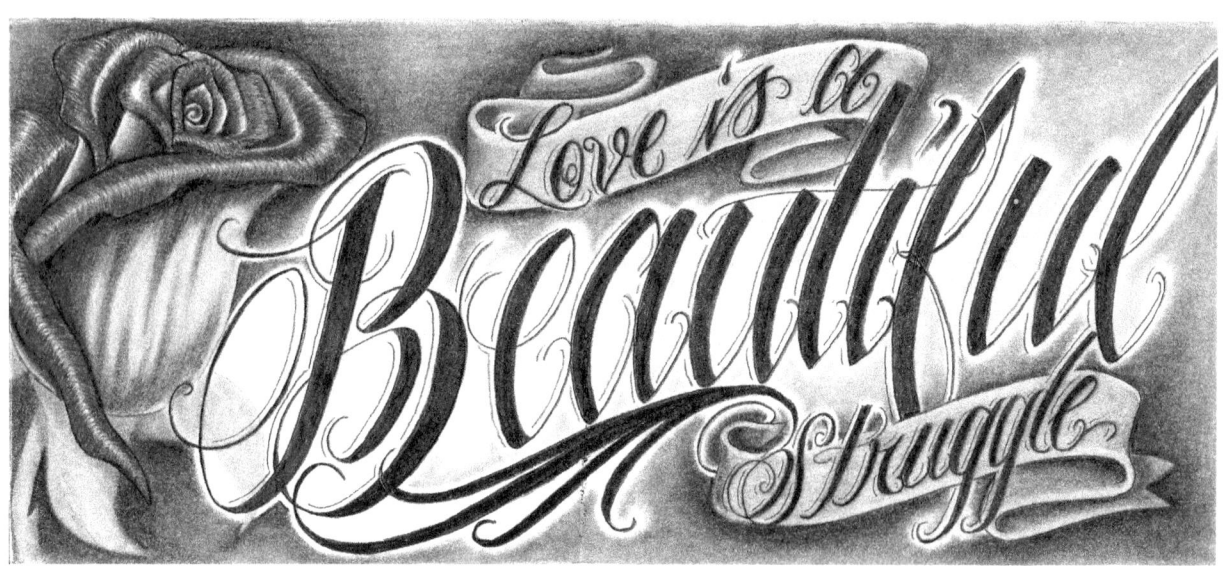

James Shaw

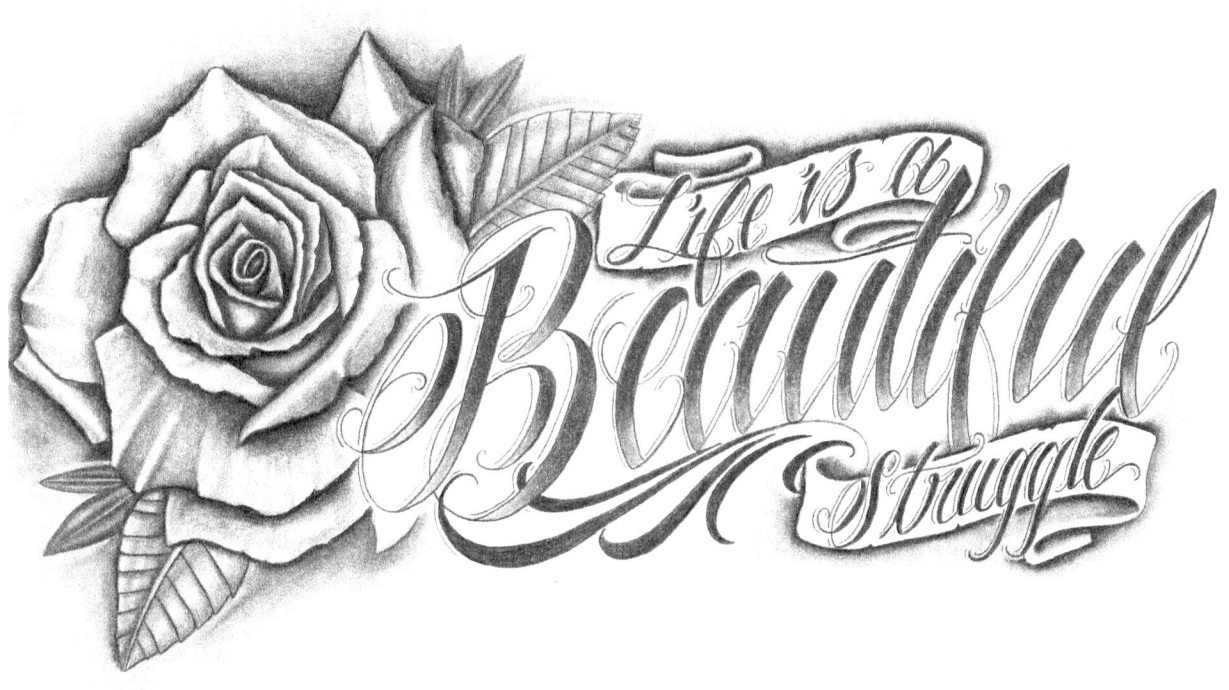

James Shaw

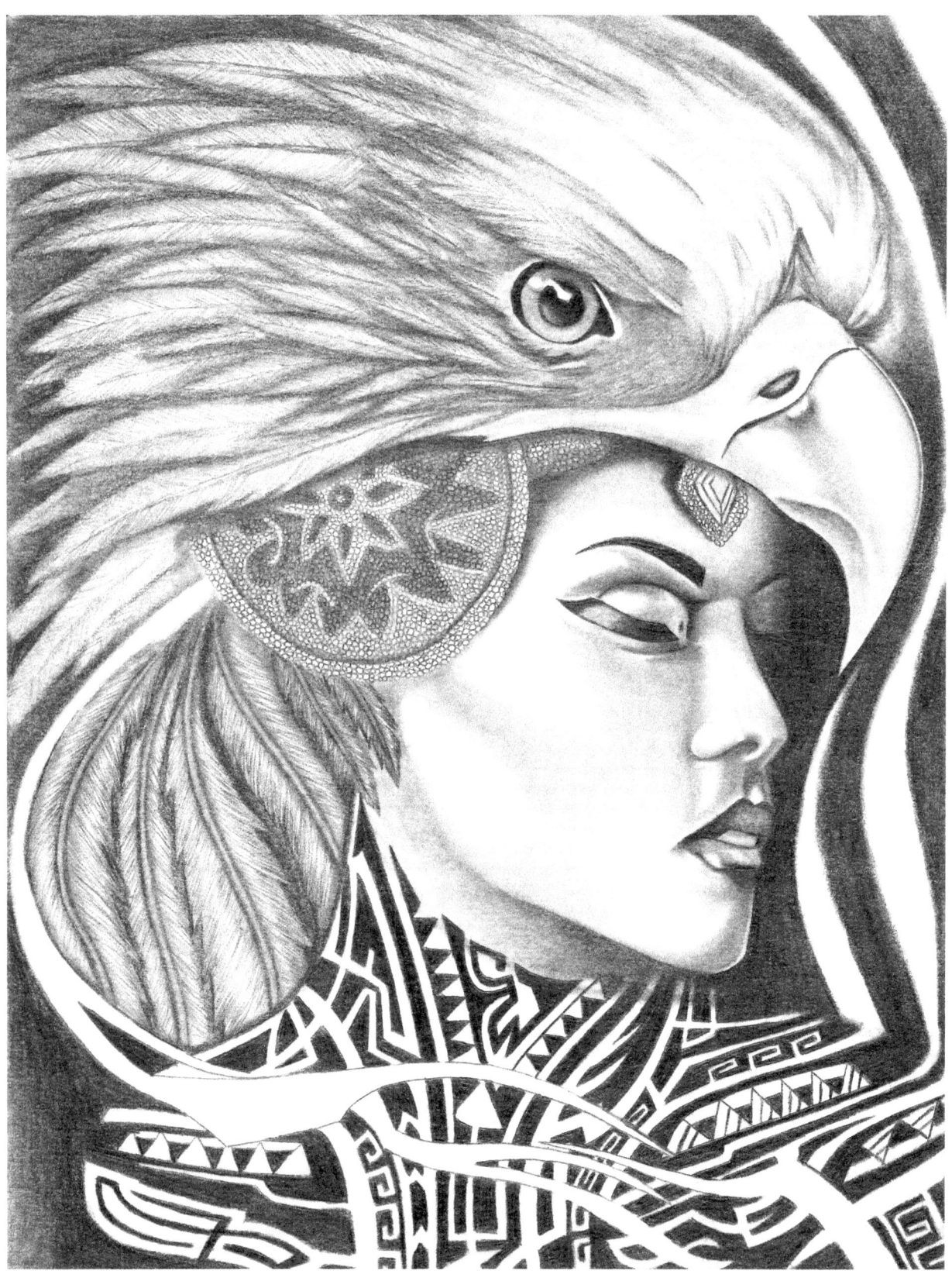

James Shaw

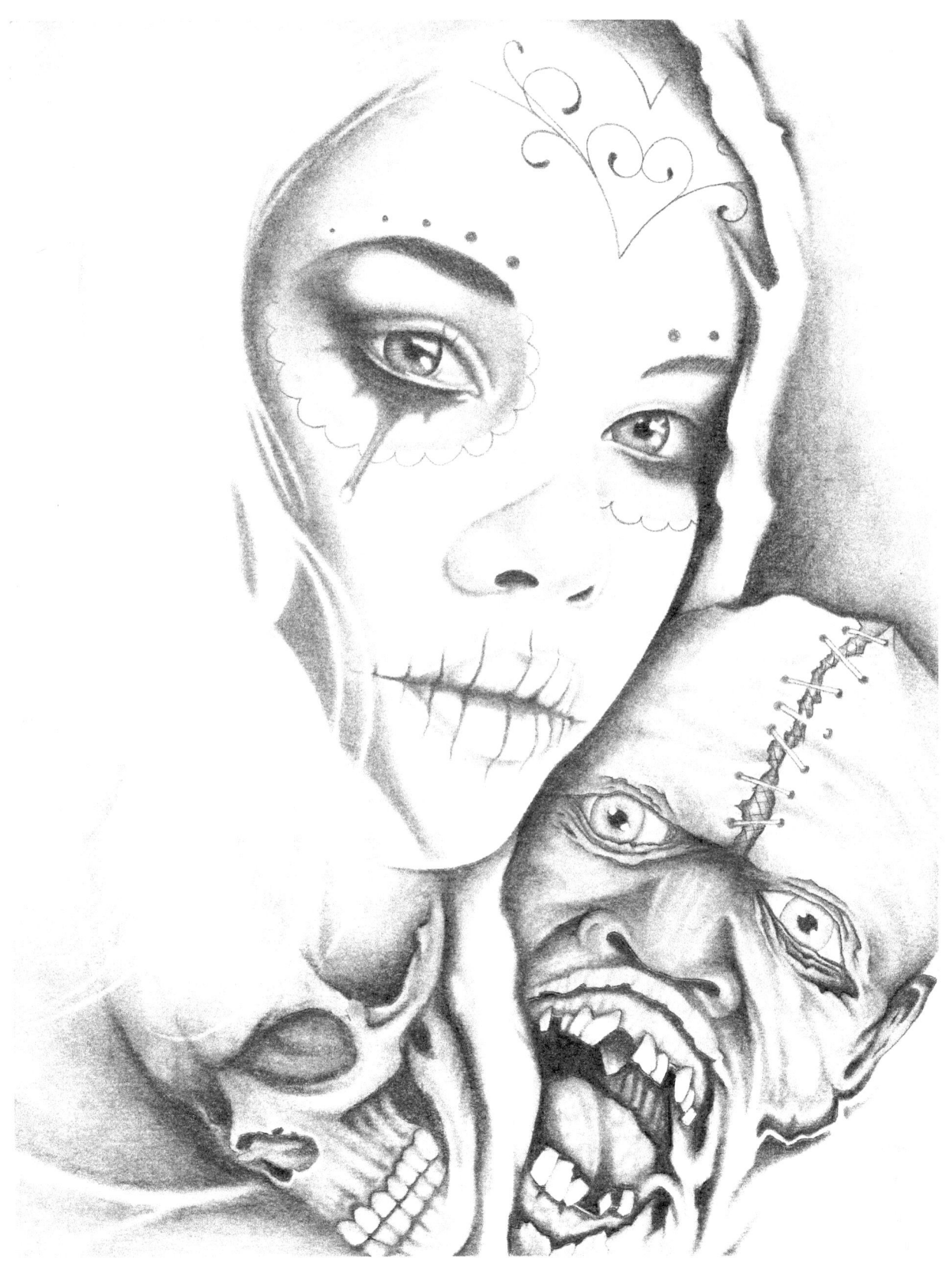

James Shaw

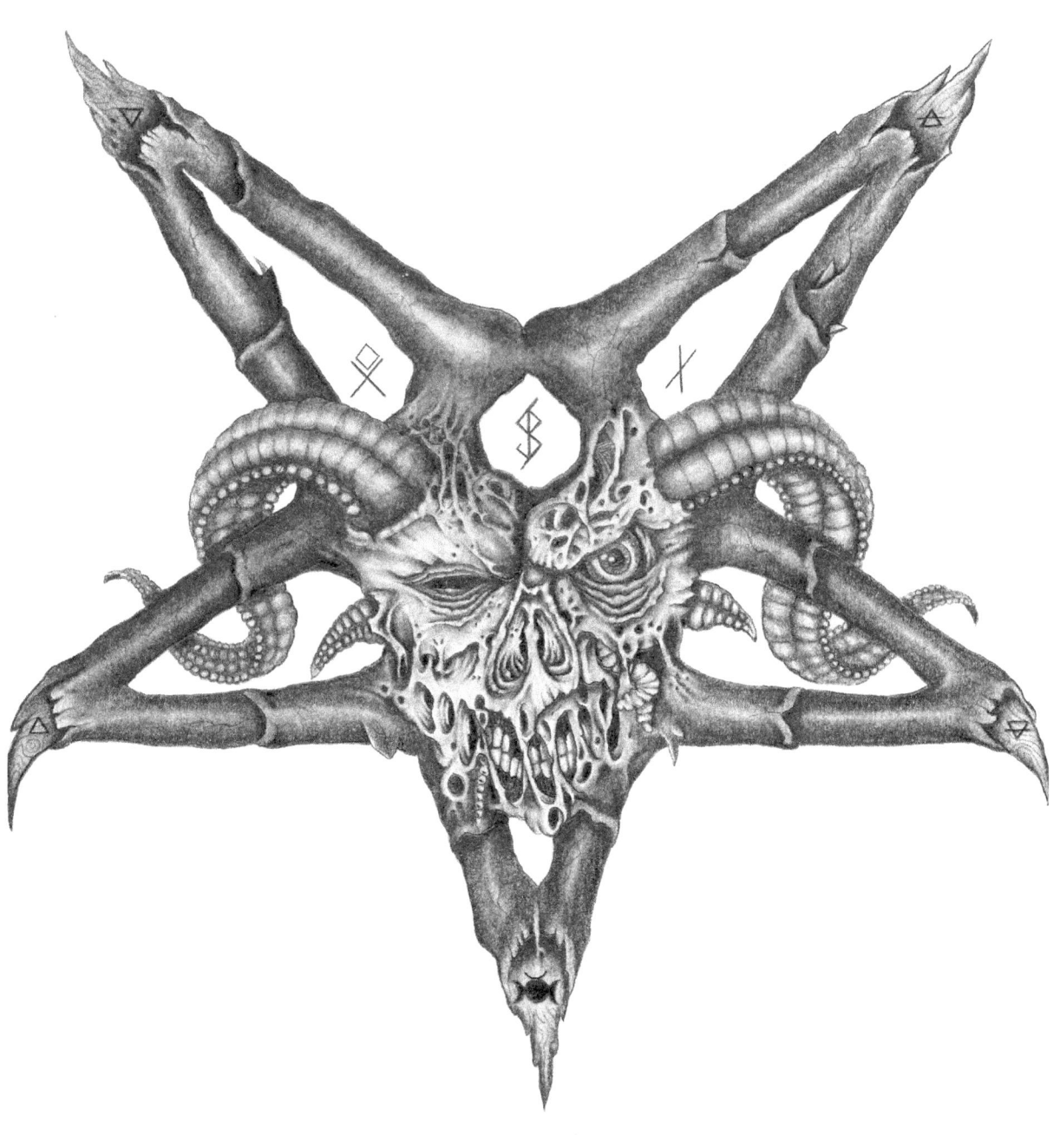

James Shaw

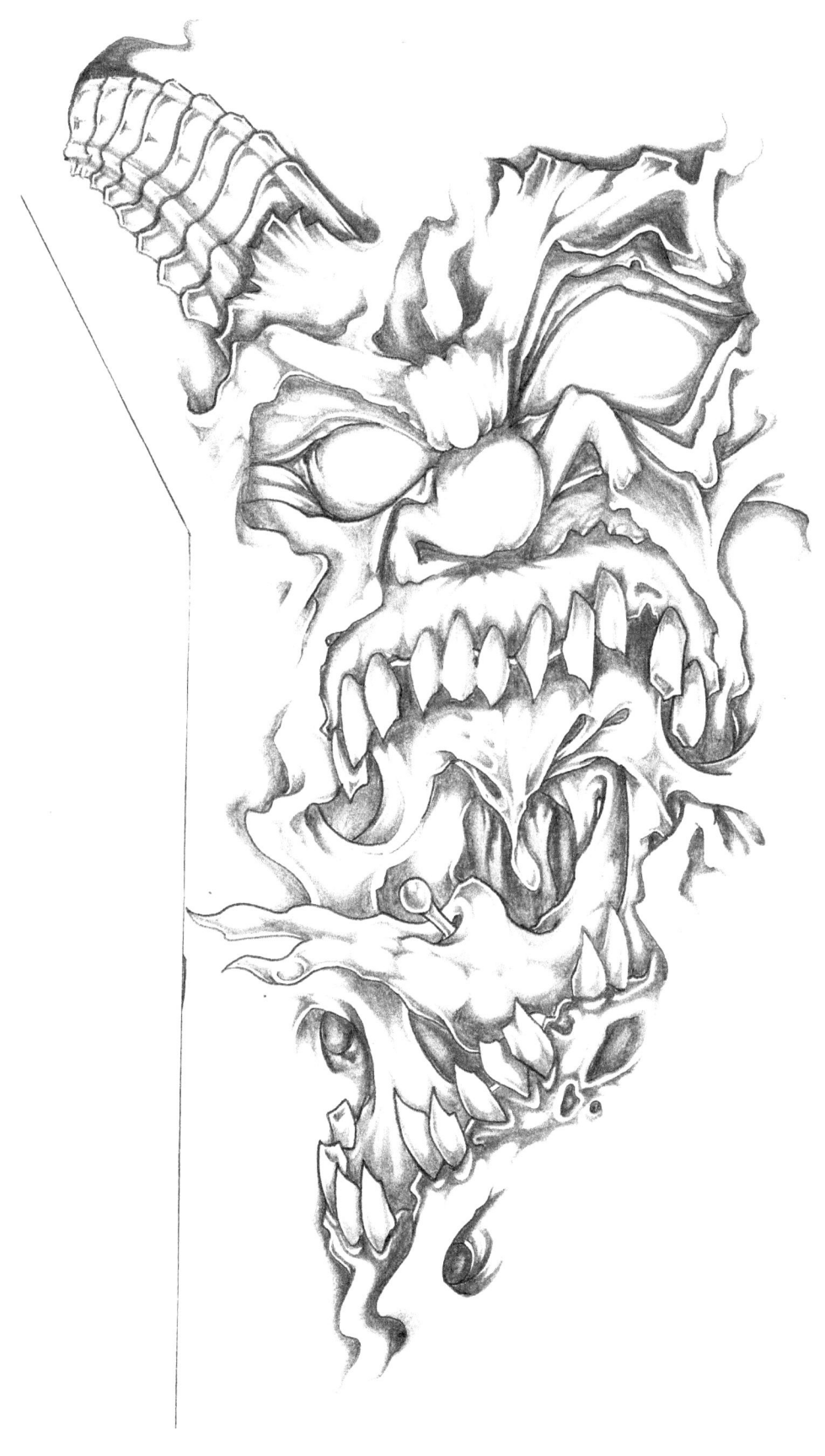

James Shaw

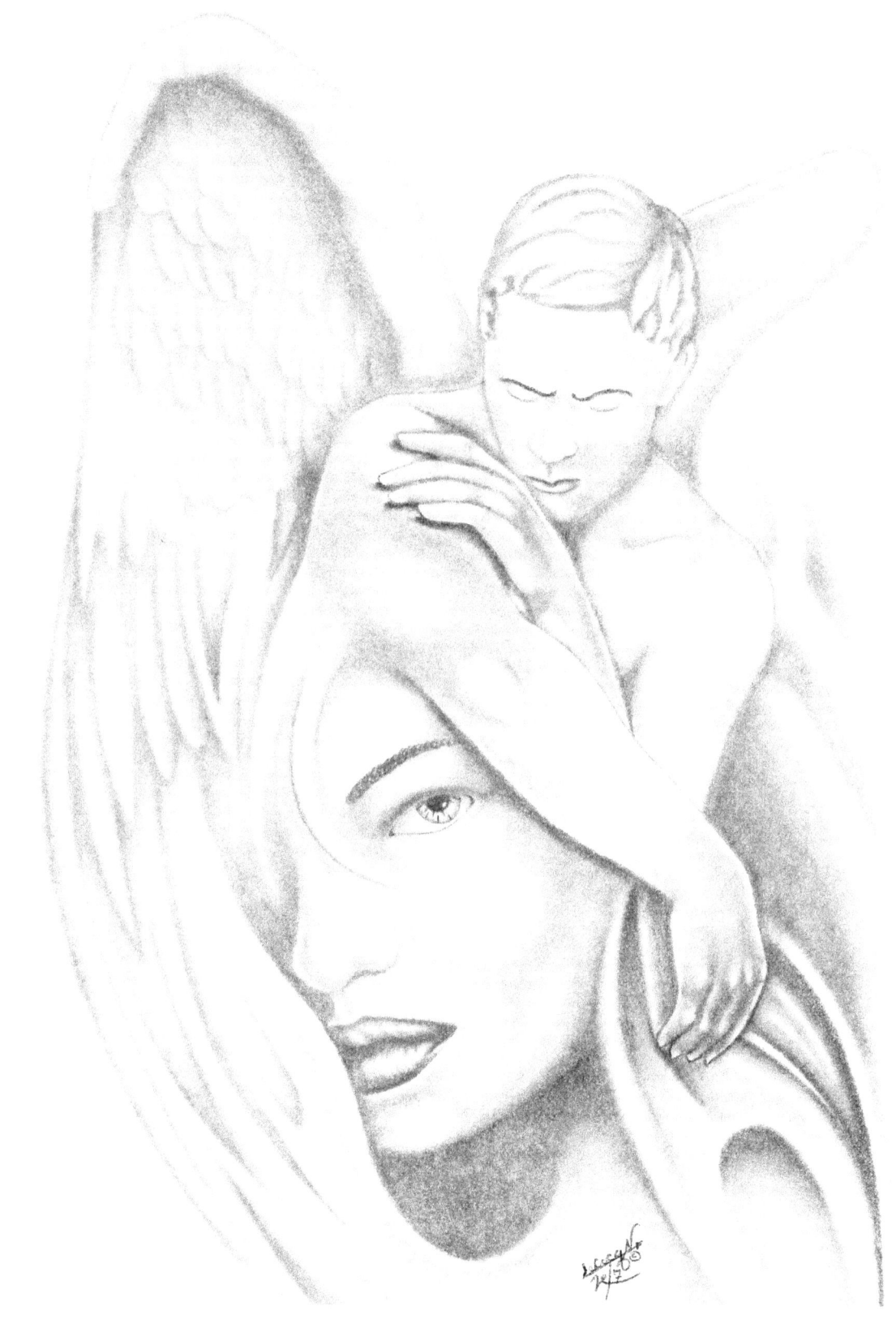

Jamie Wright

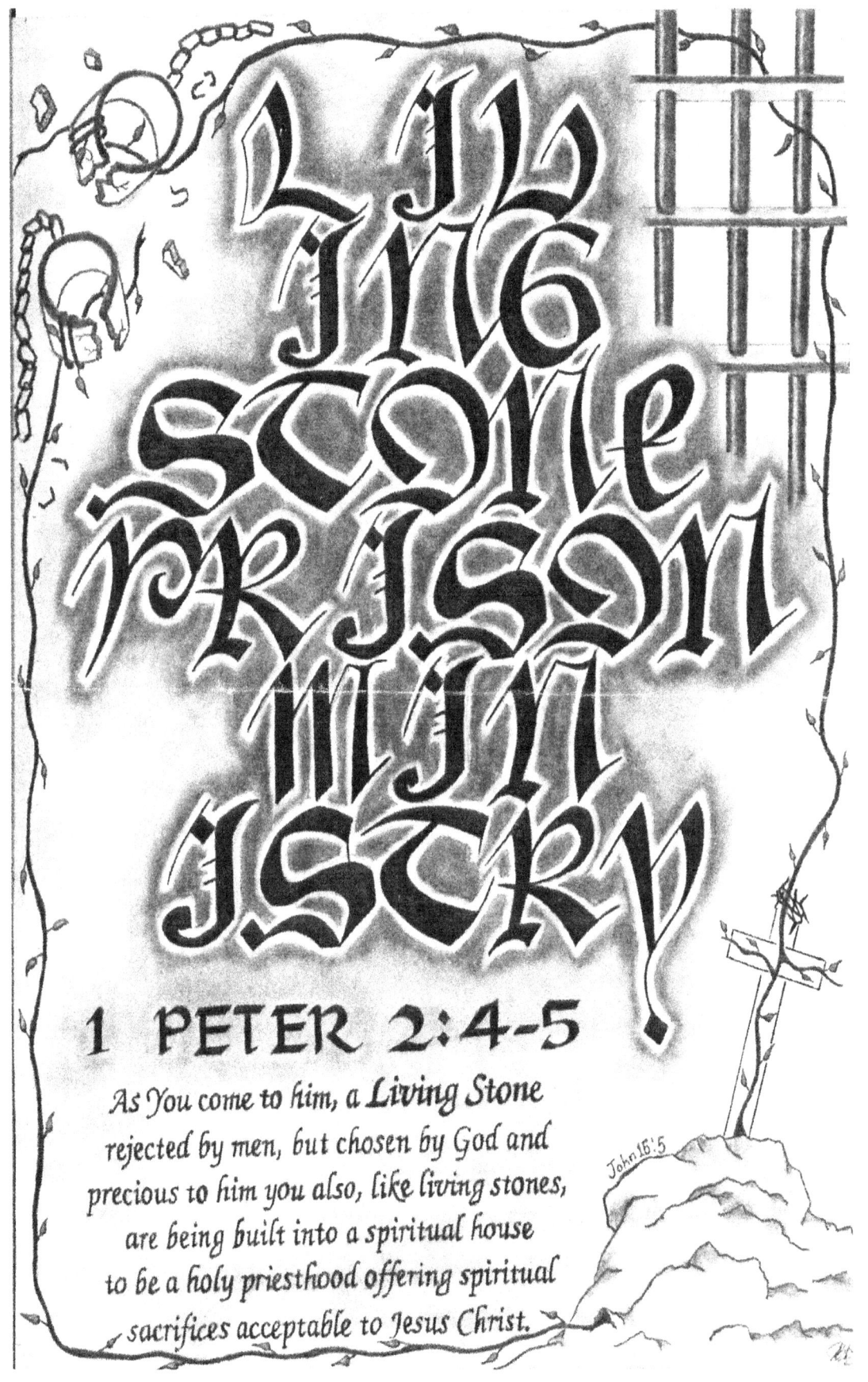

Jon Jolley

Joseph Golliher-Weyer

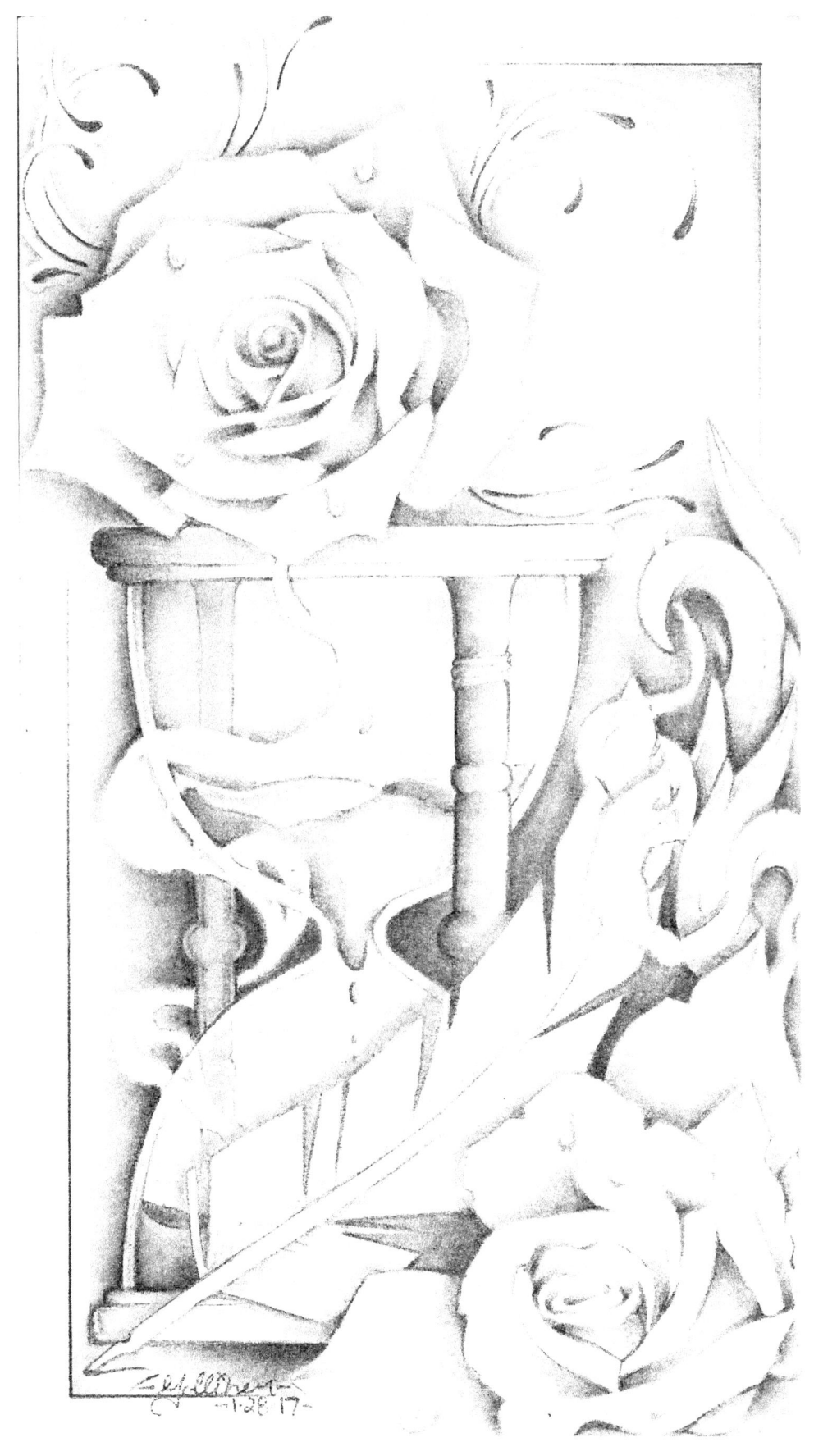

Joseph Golliher-Weyer

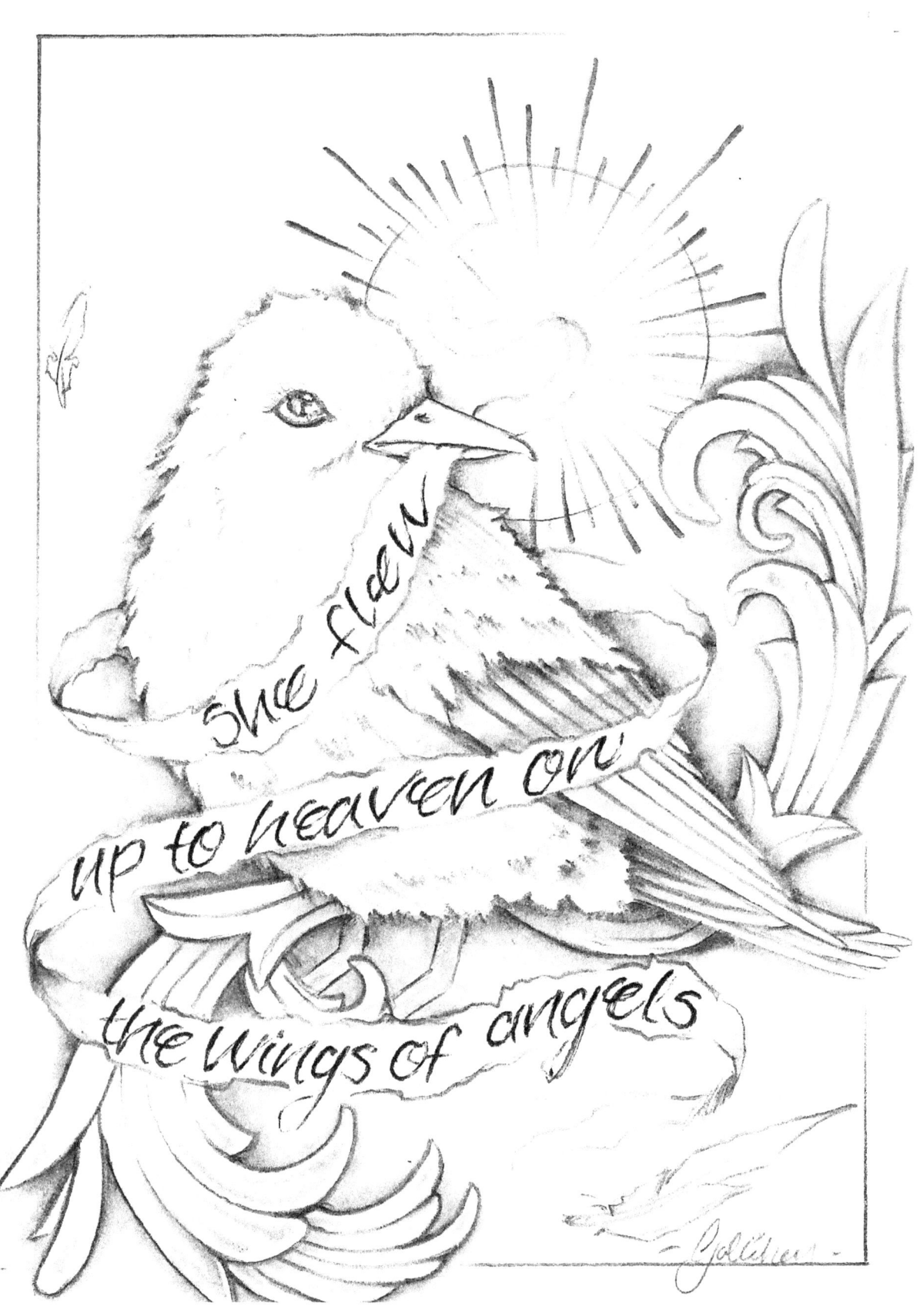

Joseph Golliher-Weyer

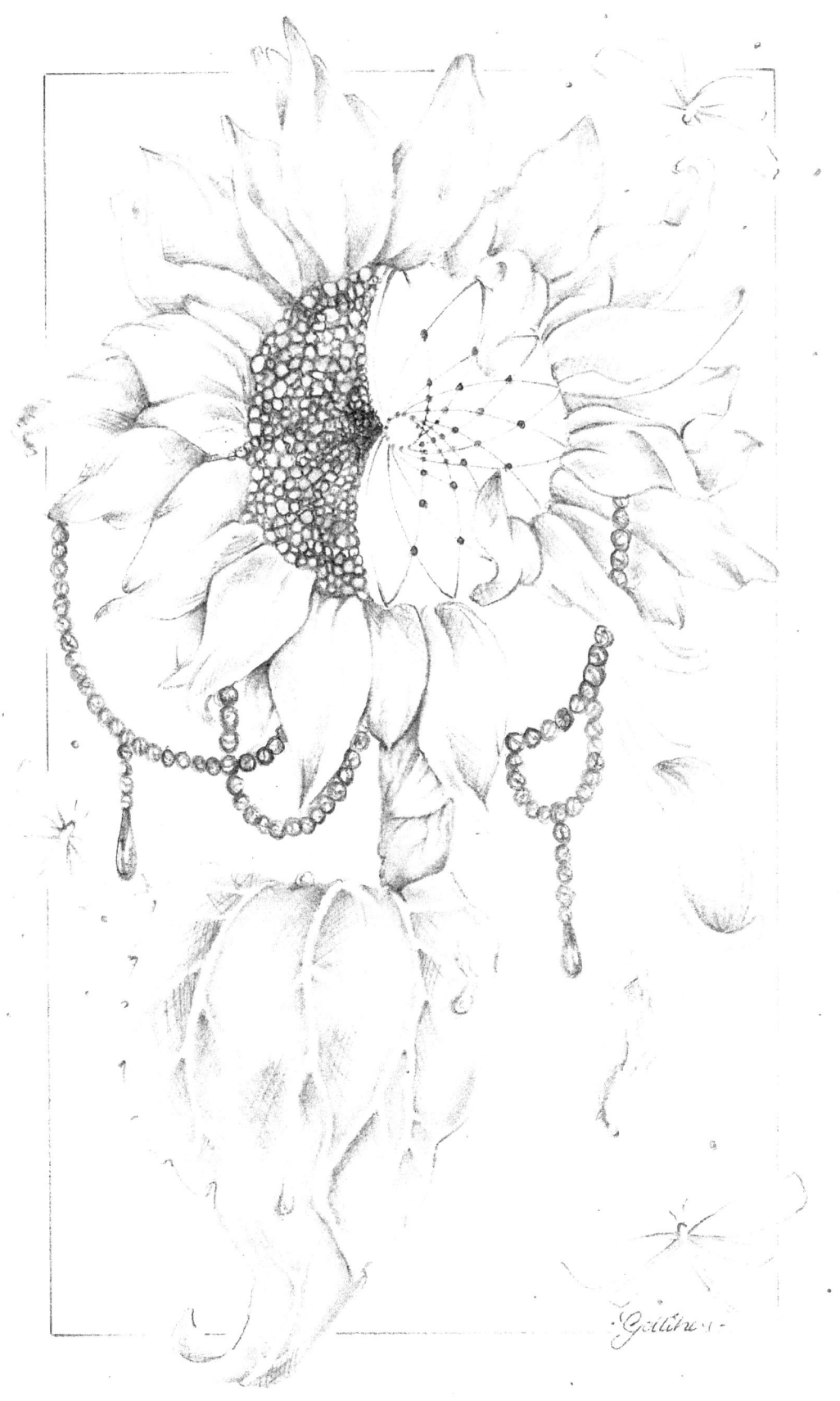

Joseph Golliher-Weyer

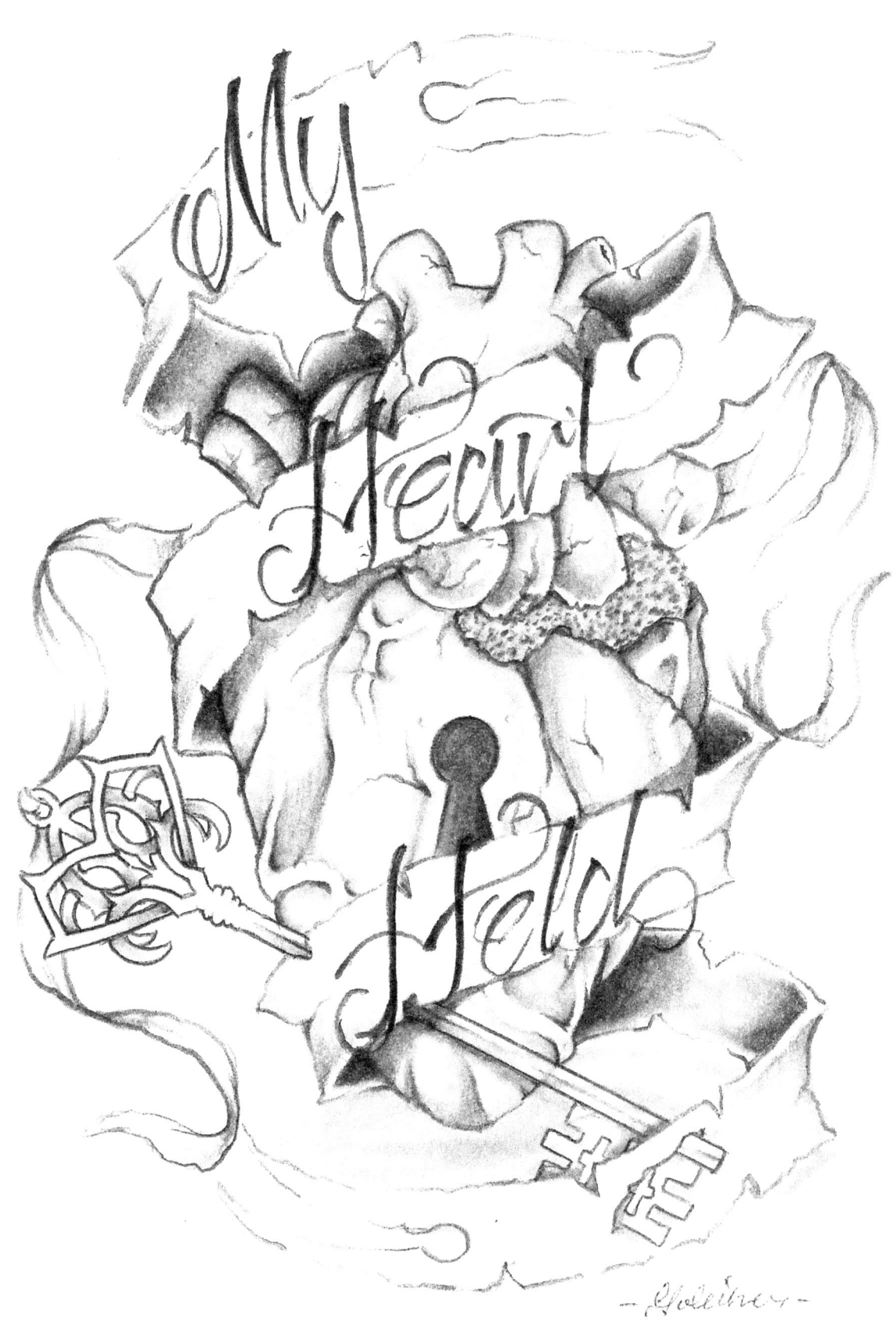

Joseph Golliher-Weyer

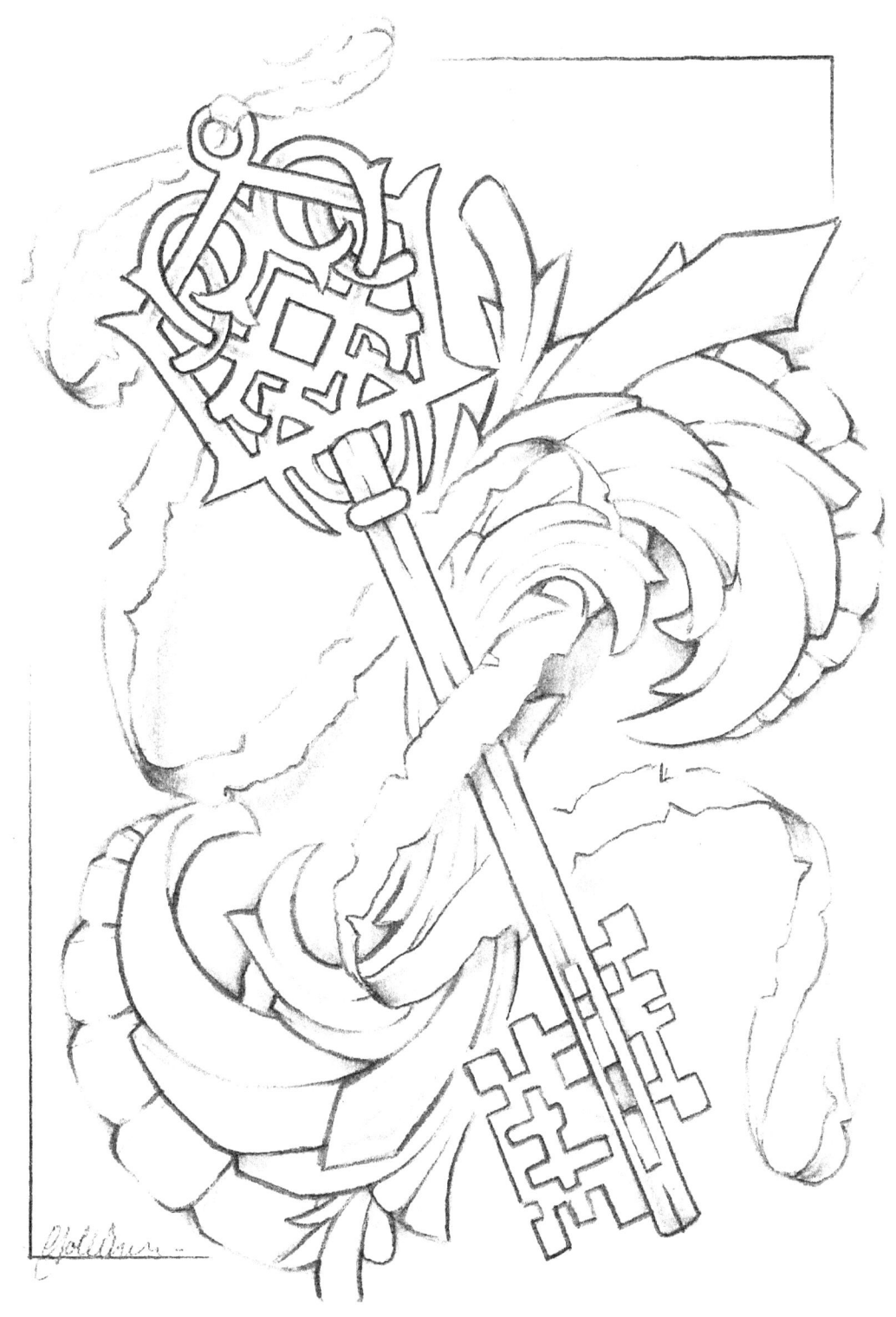

Michael Sedlmeier

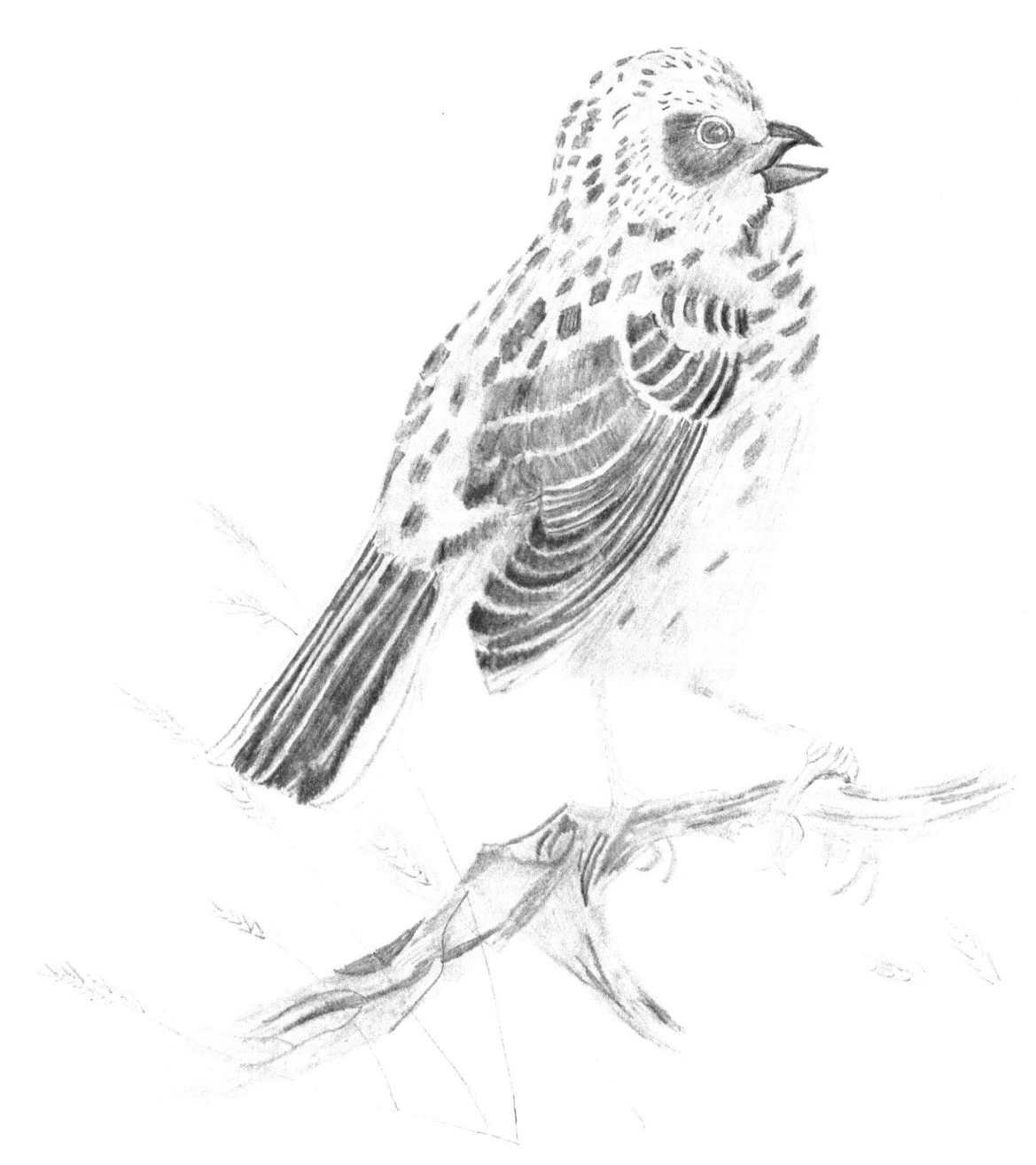

Michael Sedlmeier

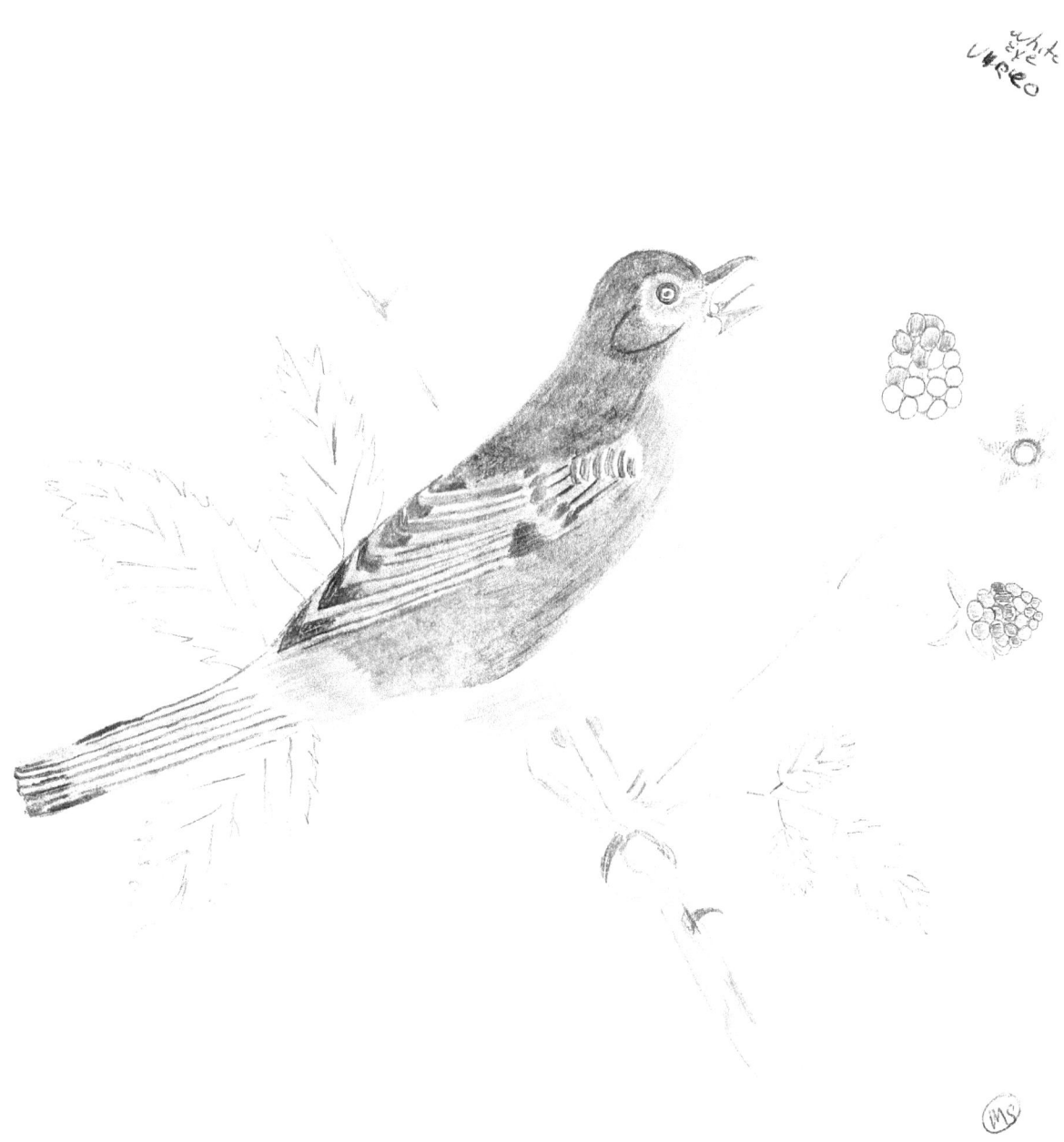

Michael Sedlmeier

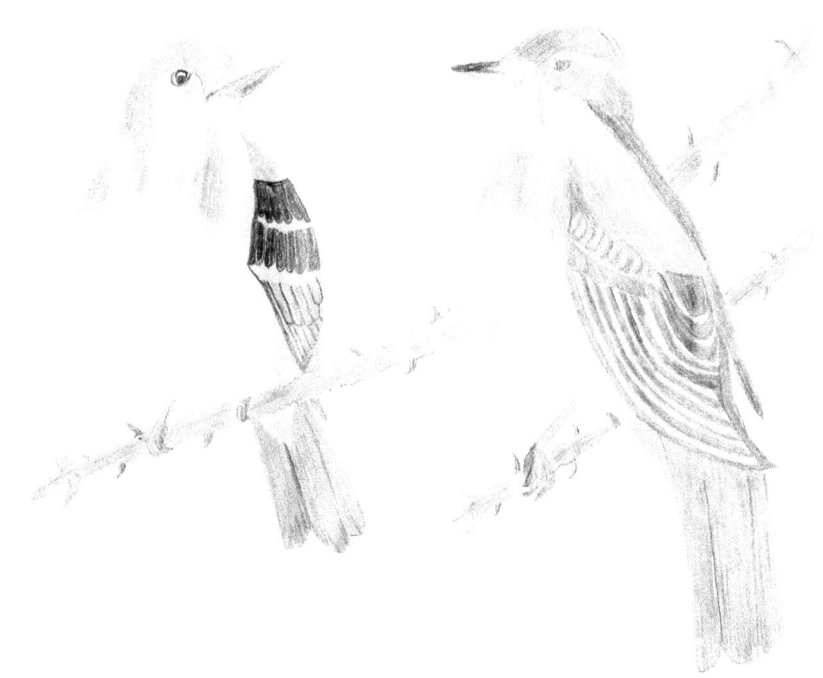

Yellow Bellied Flycatcher

Paul Wentzel

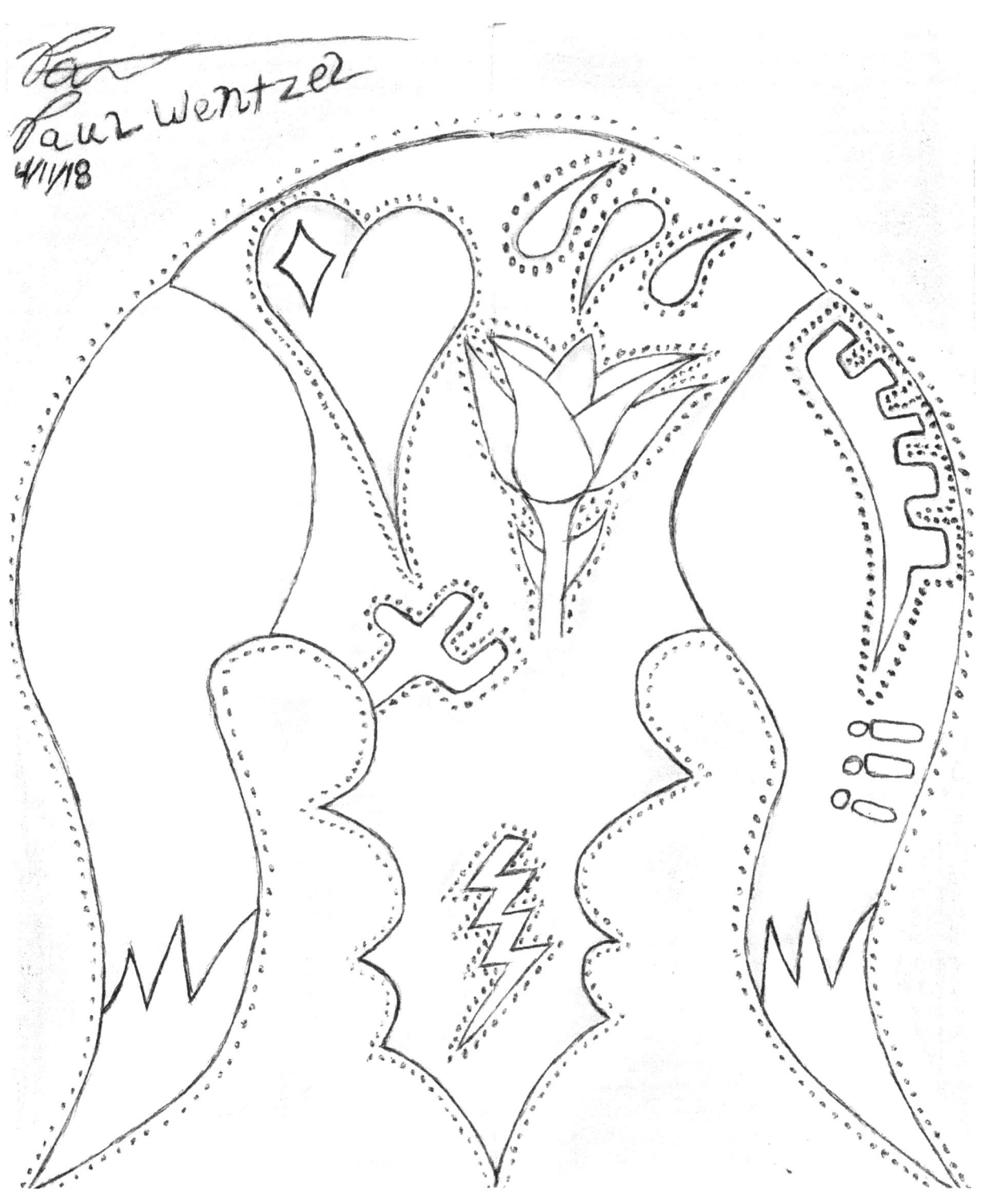

Richard Traversie

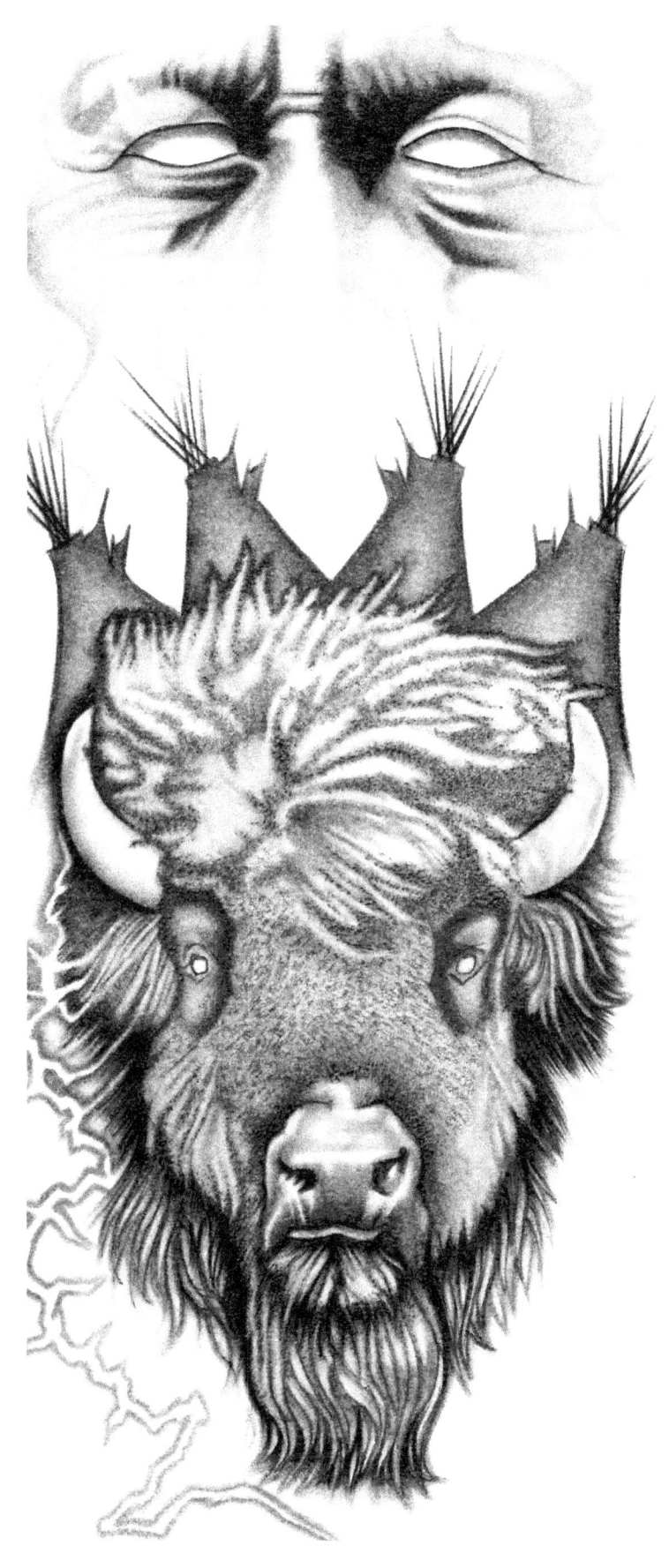

Richard Traversie

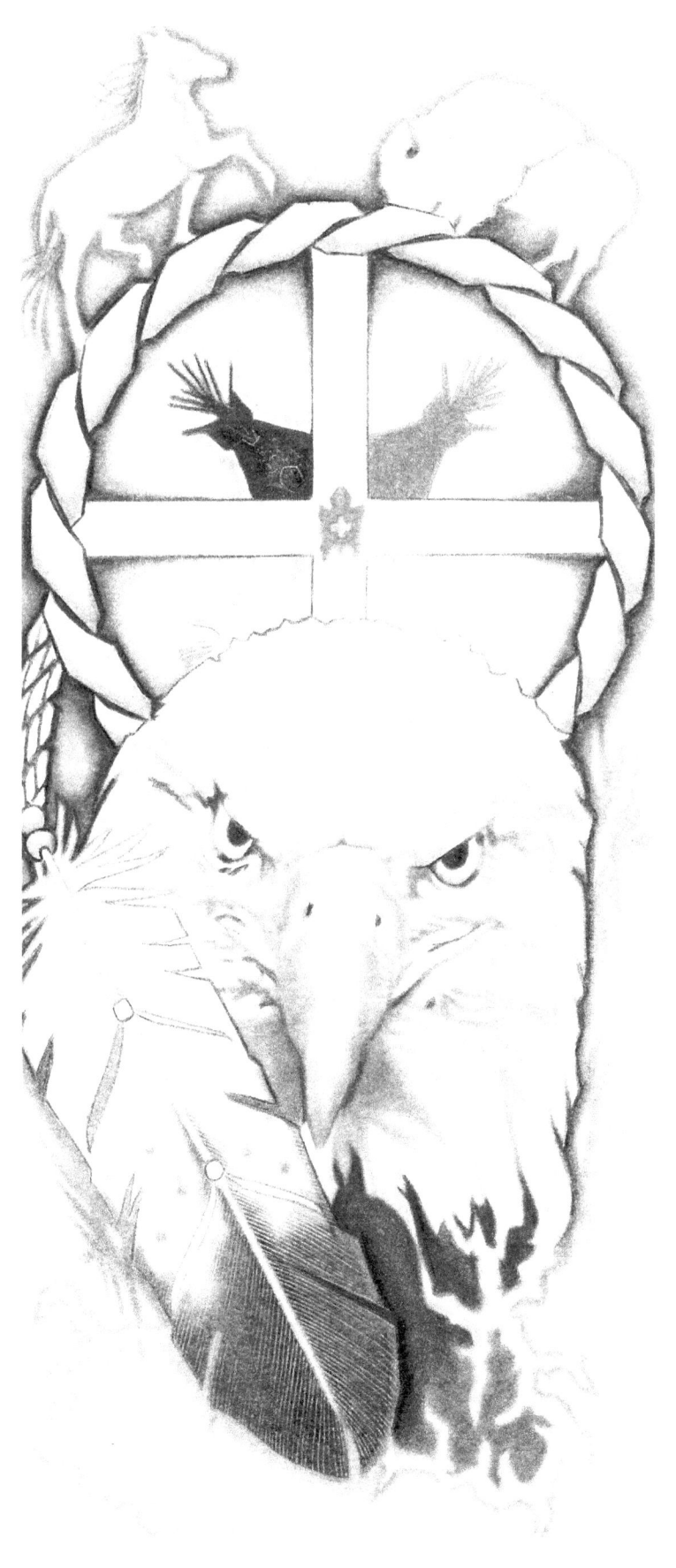

Richard Traversie

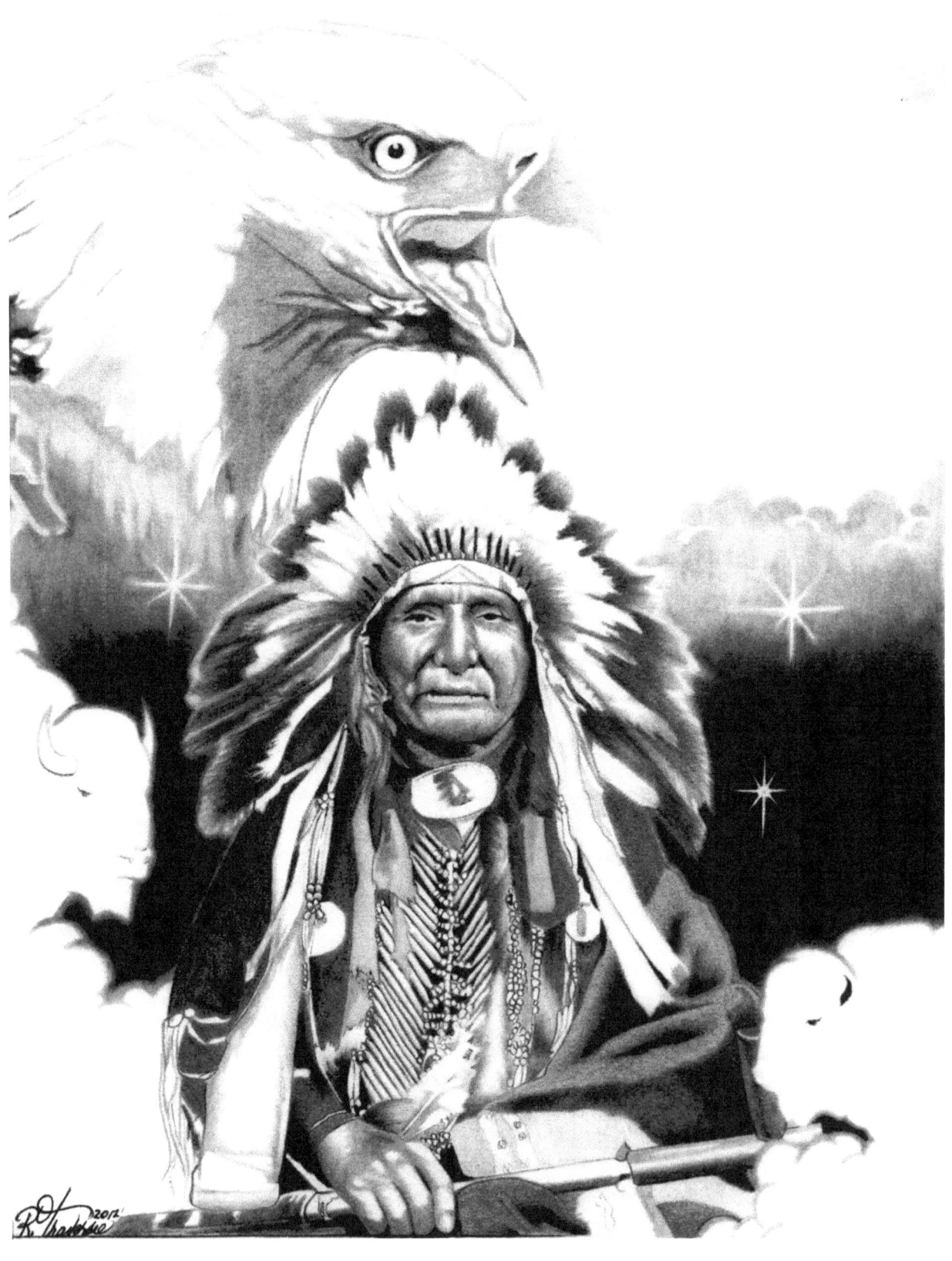

Richard Traversie

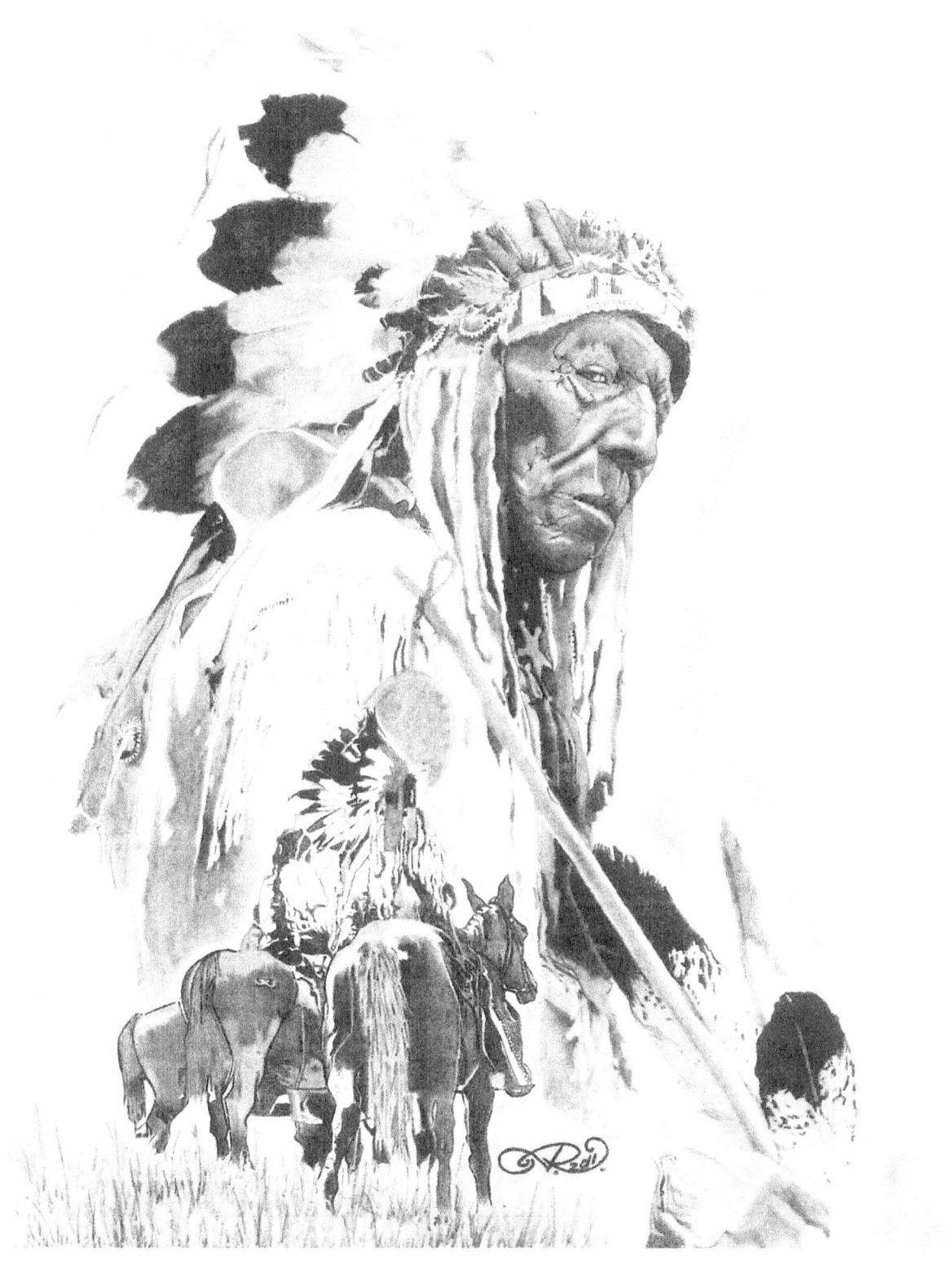

Richard Traversie

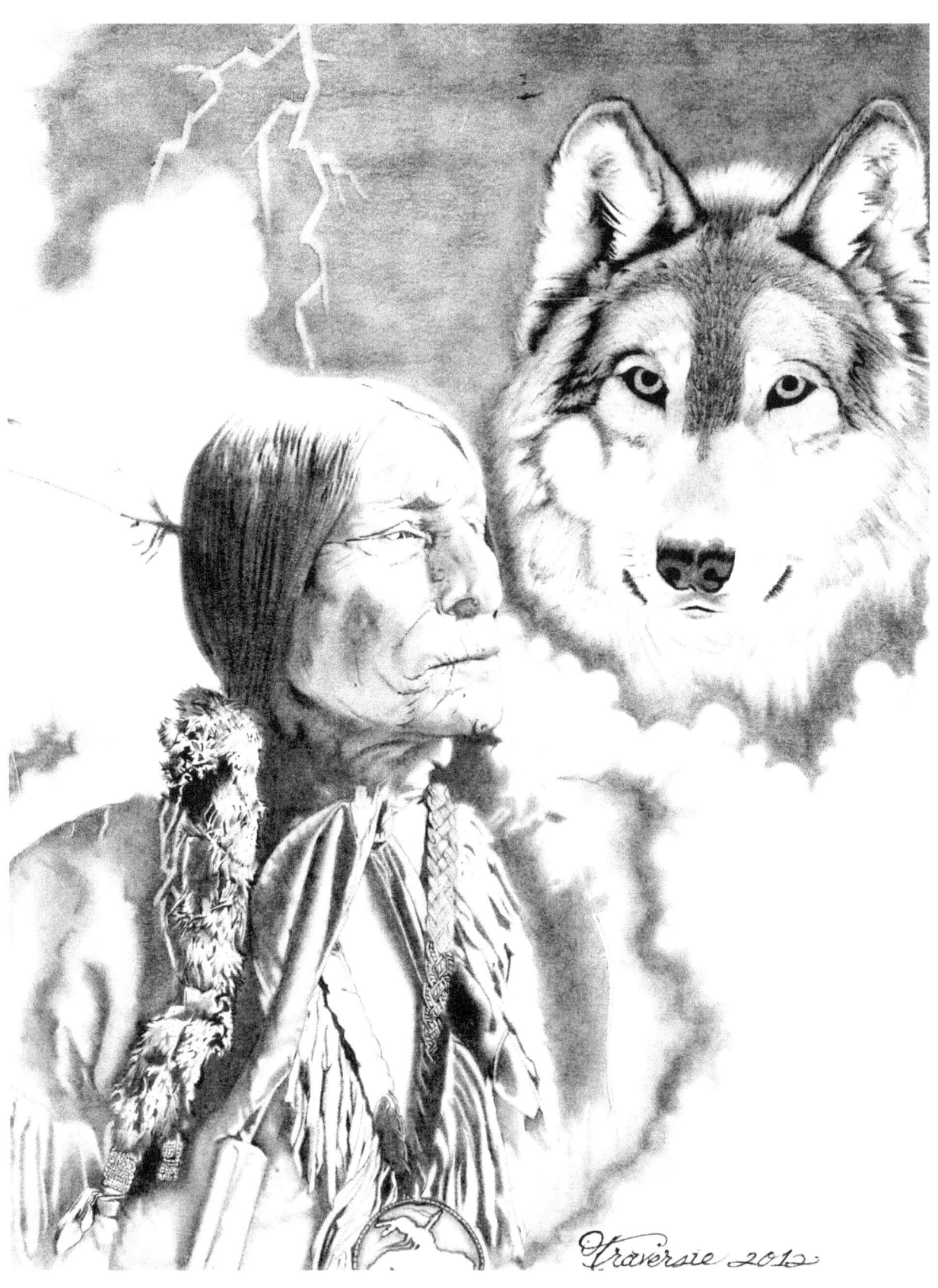

Richard Traversie

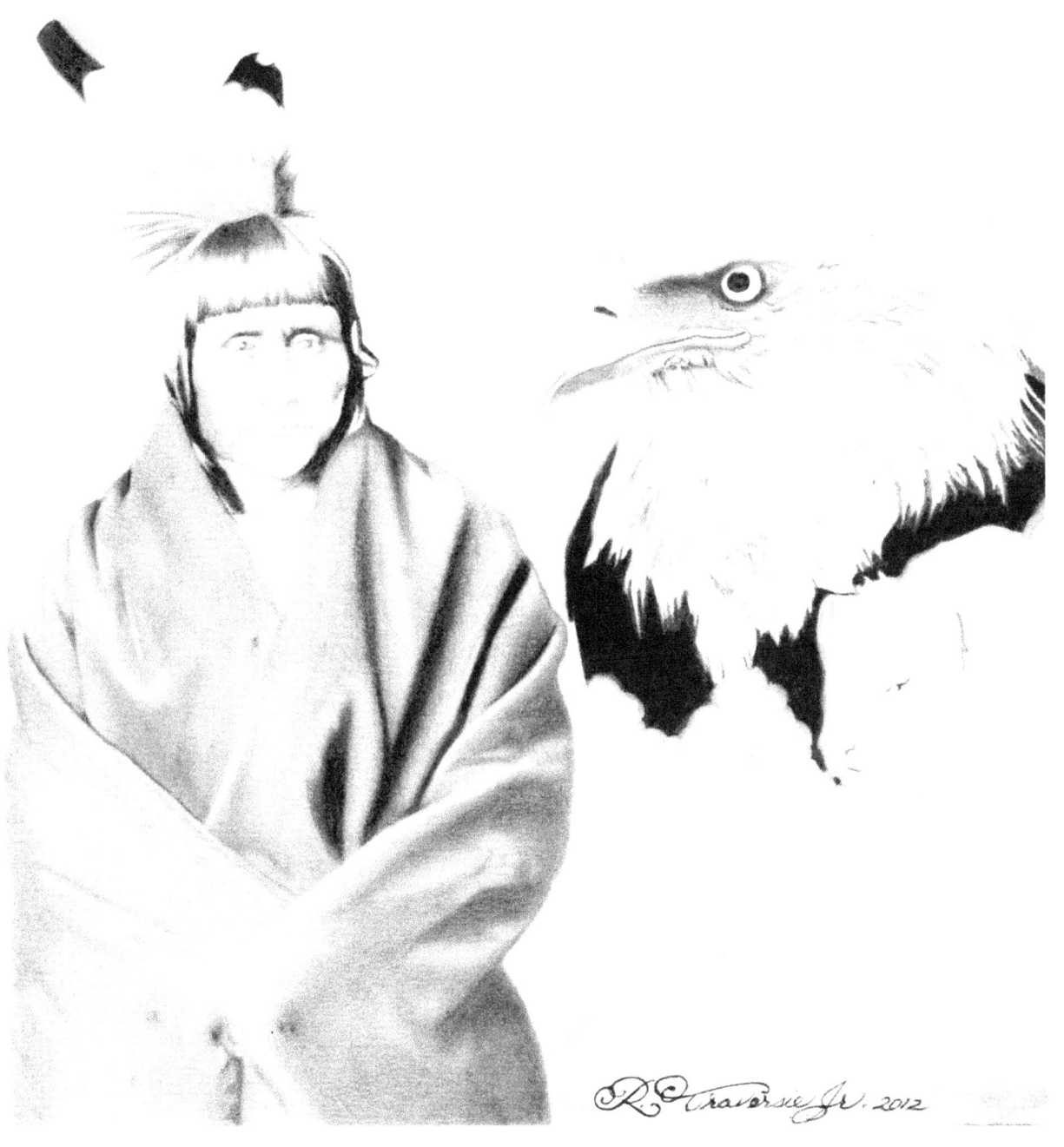

Richard Traversie

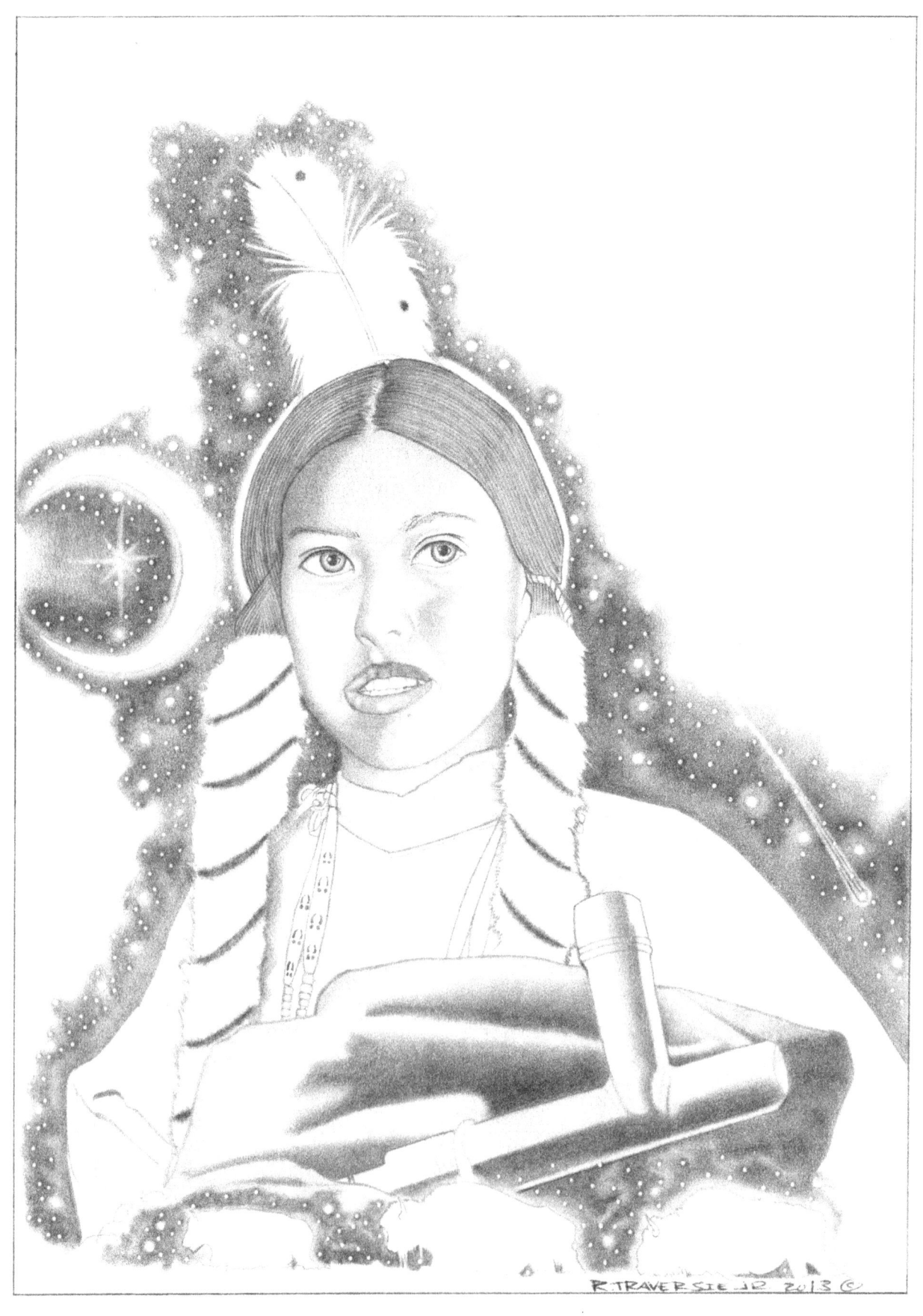

Richard Traversie

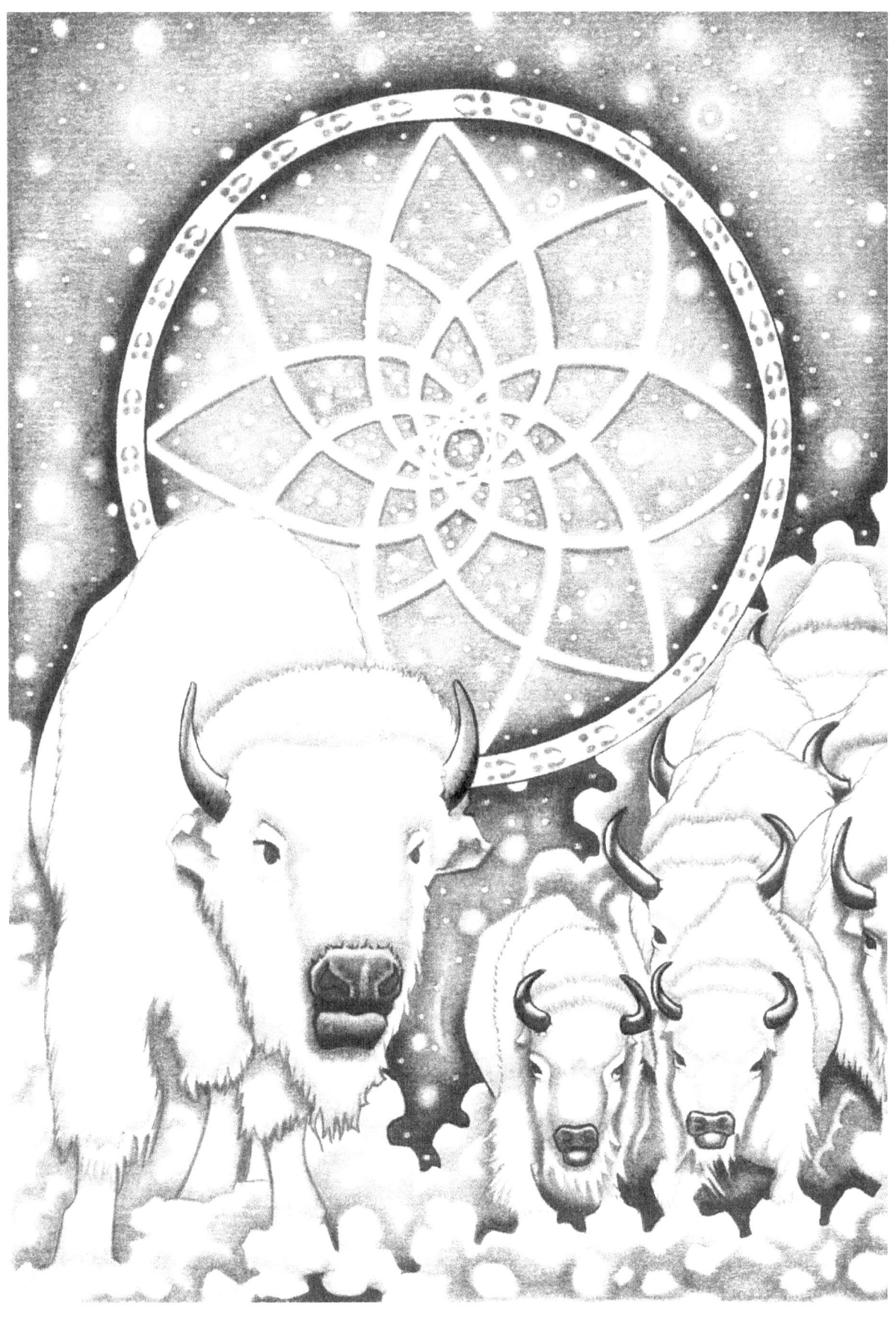

Shane Archer

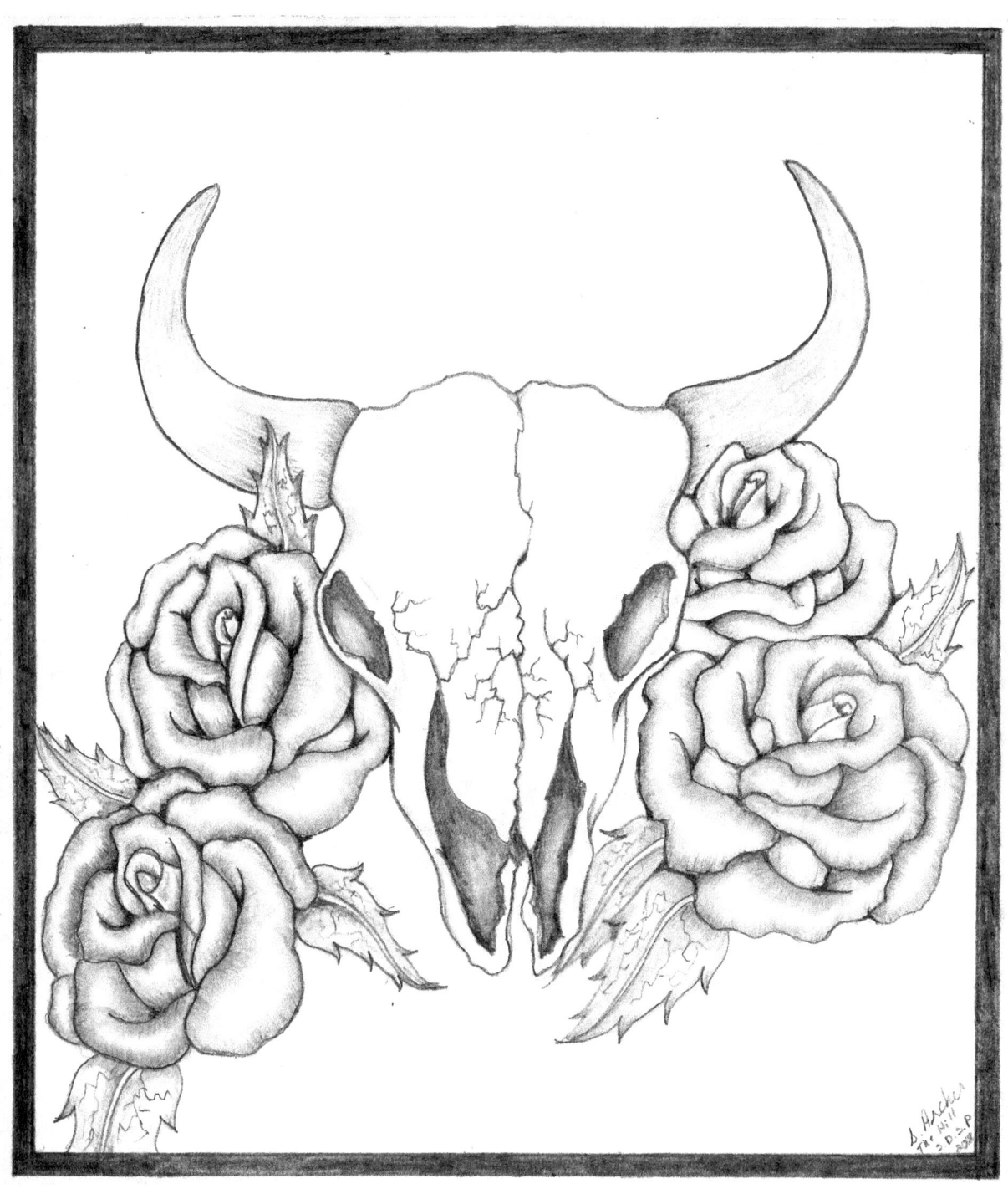

Shane Archer

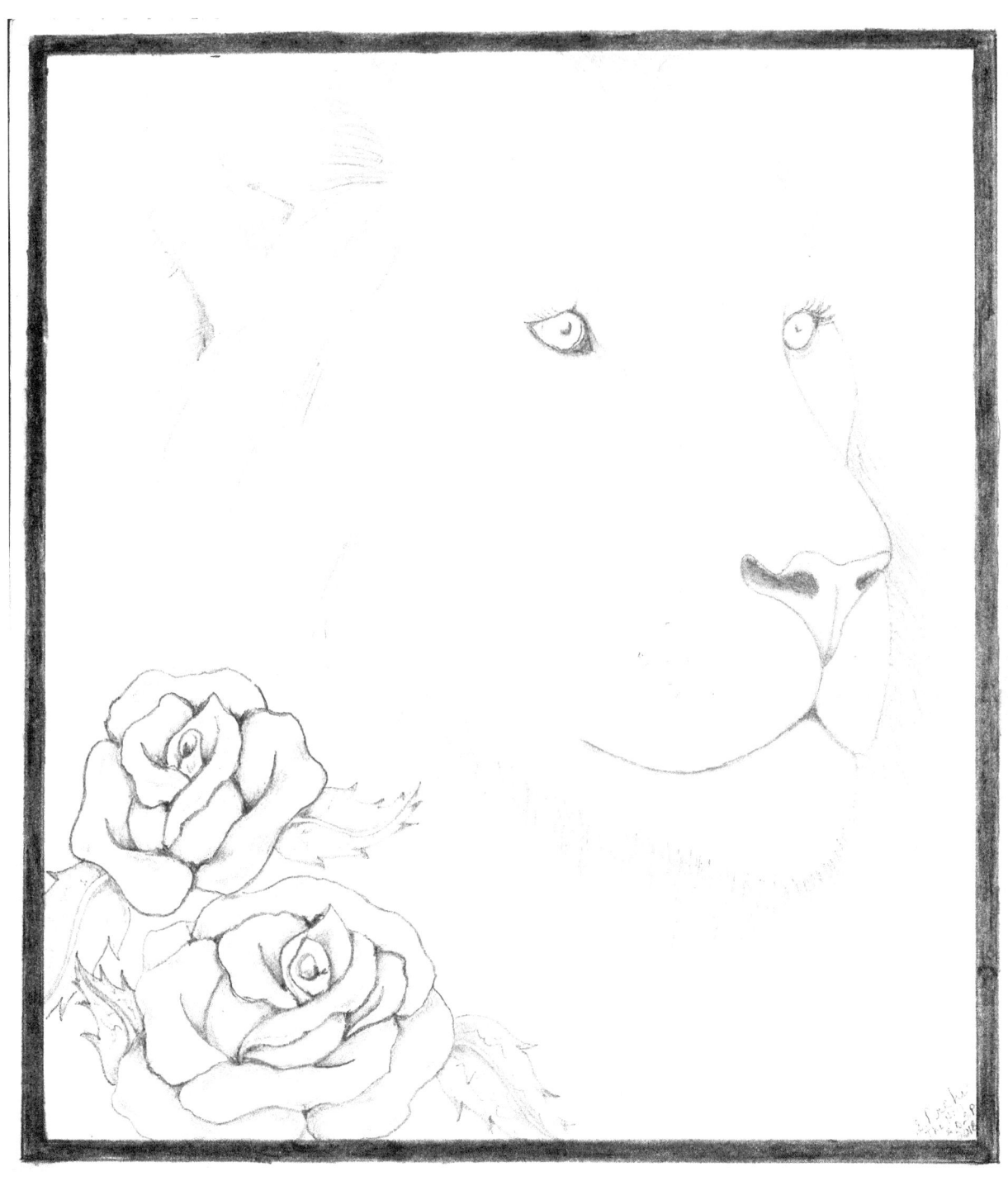

Shane Archer

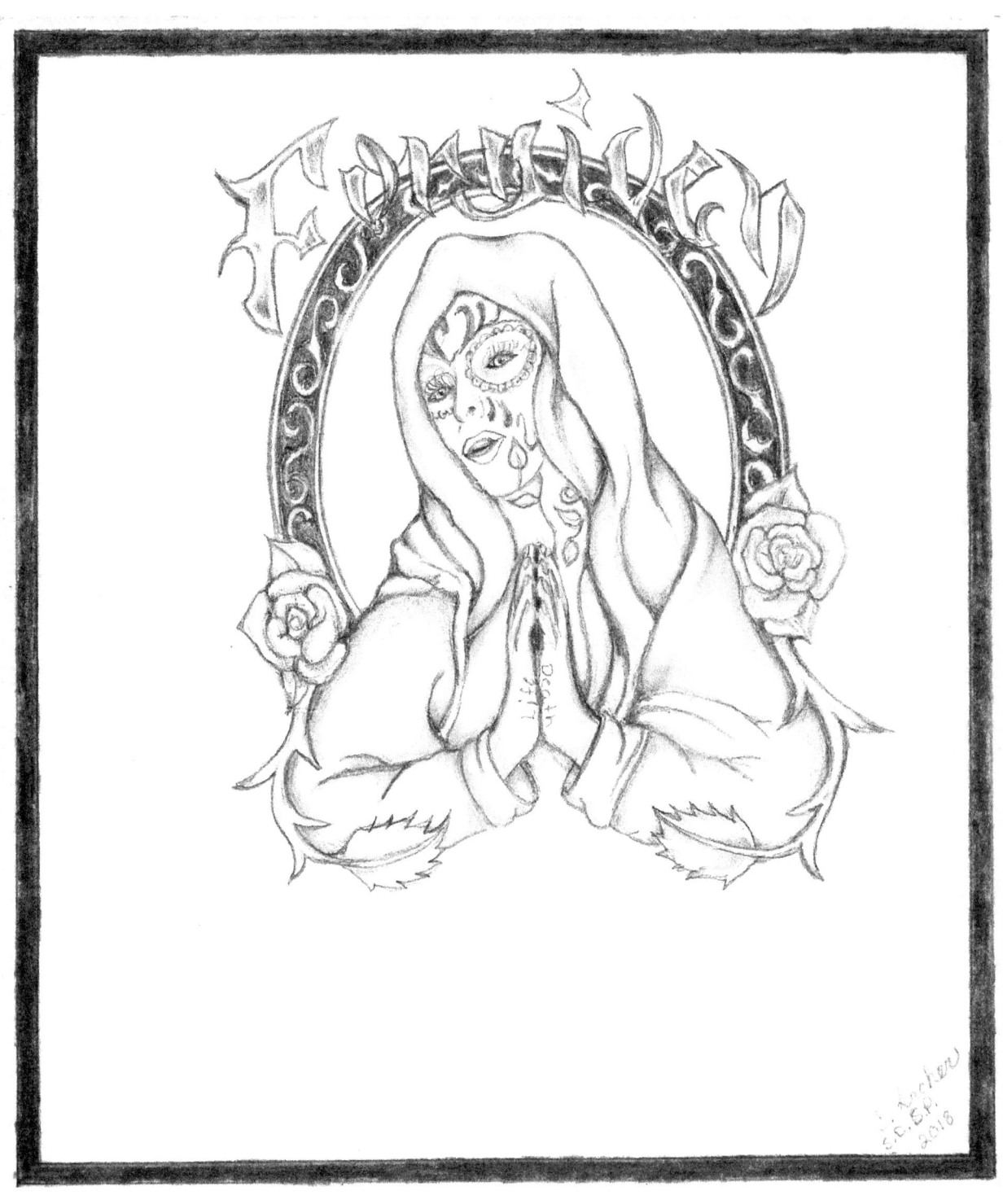

Shane Archer

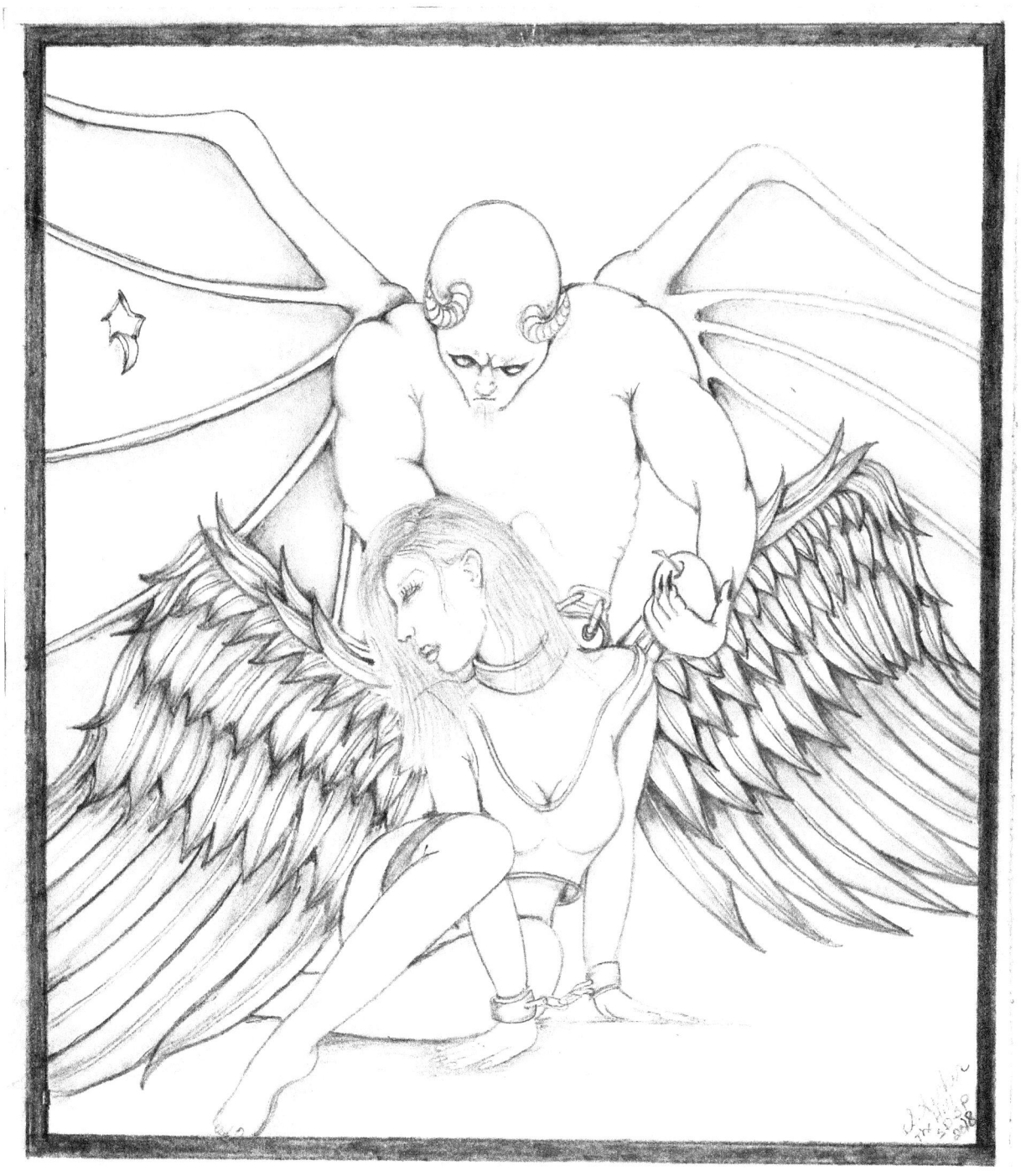

Shane Archer

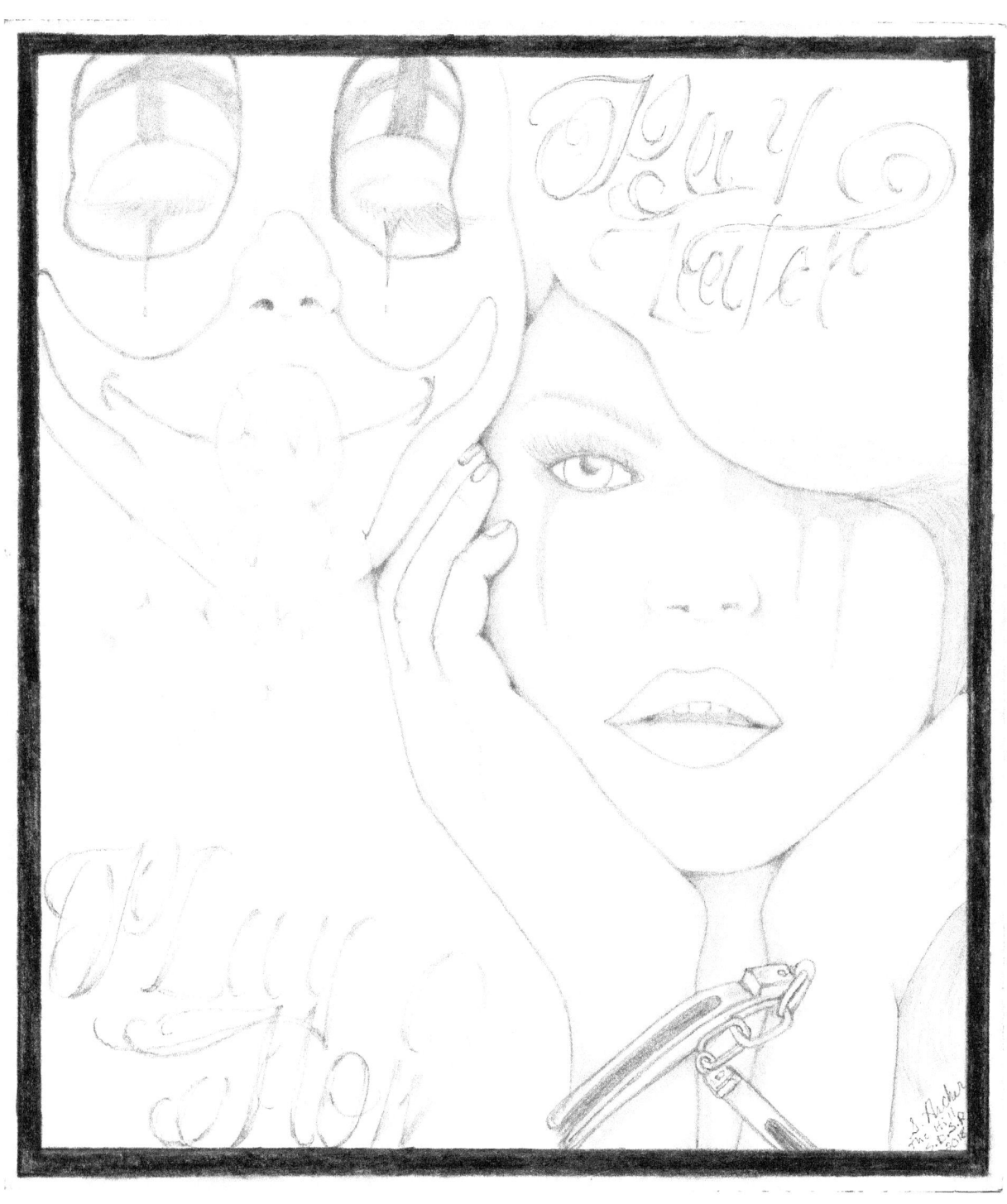

Shane Archer

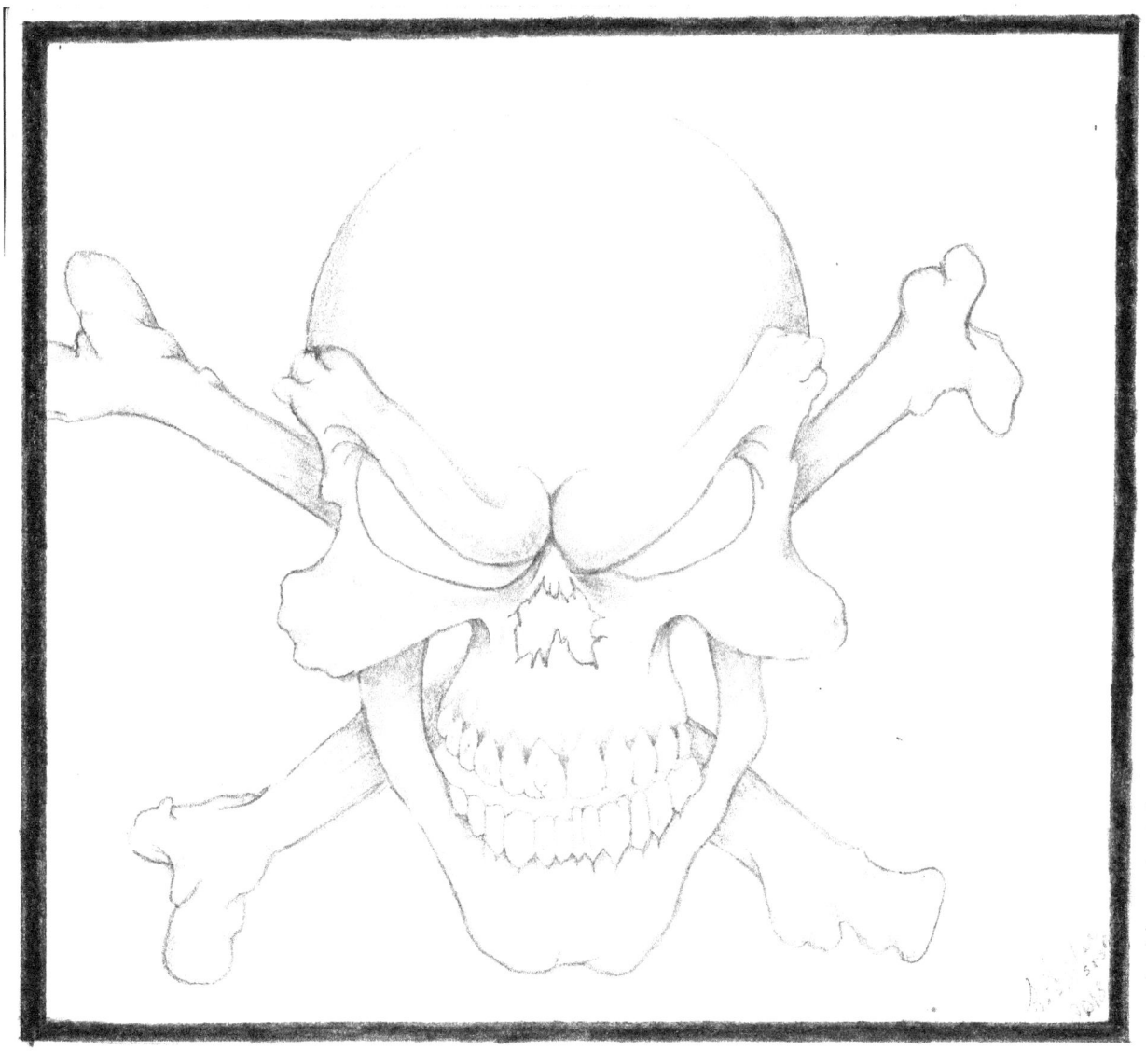

Shane Archer

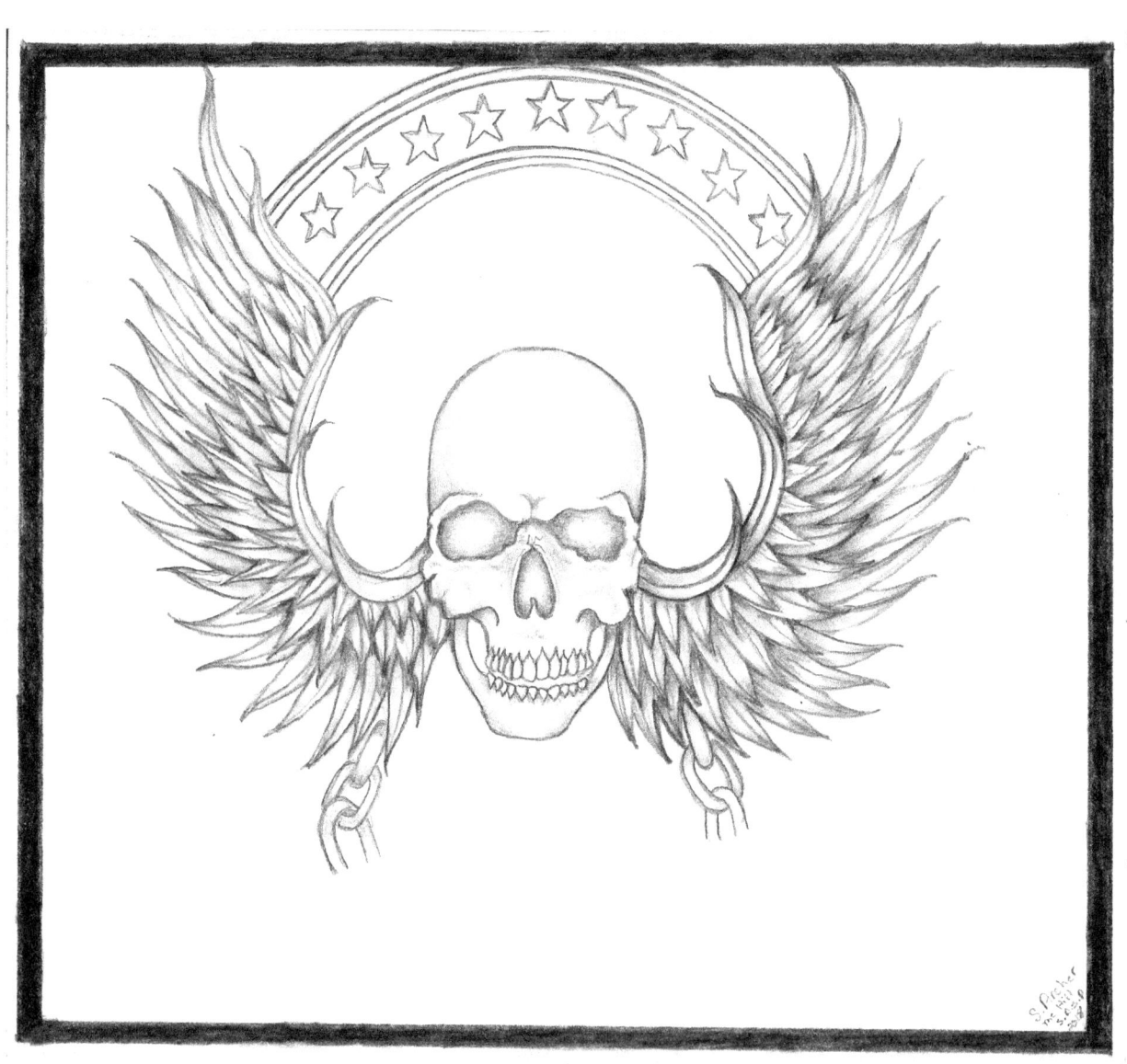

Shane Archer

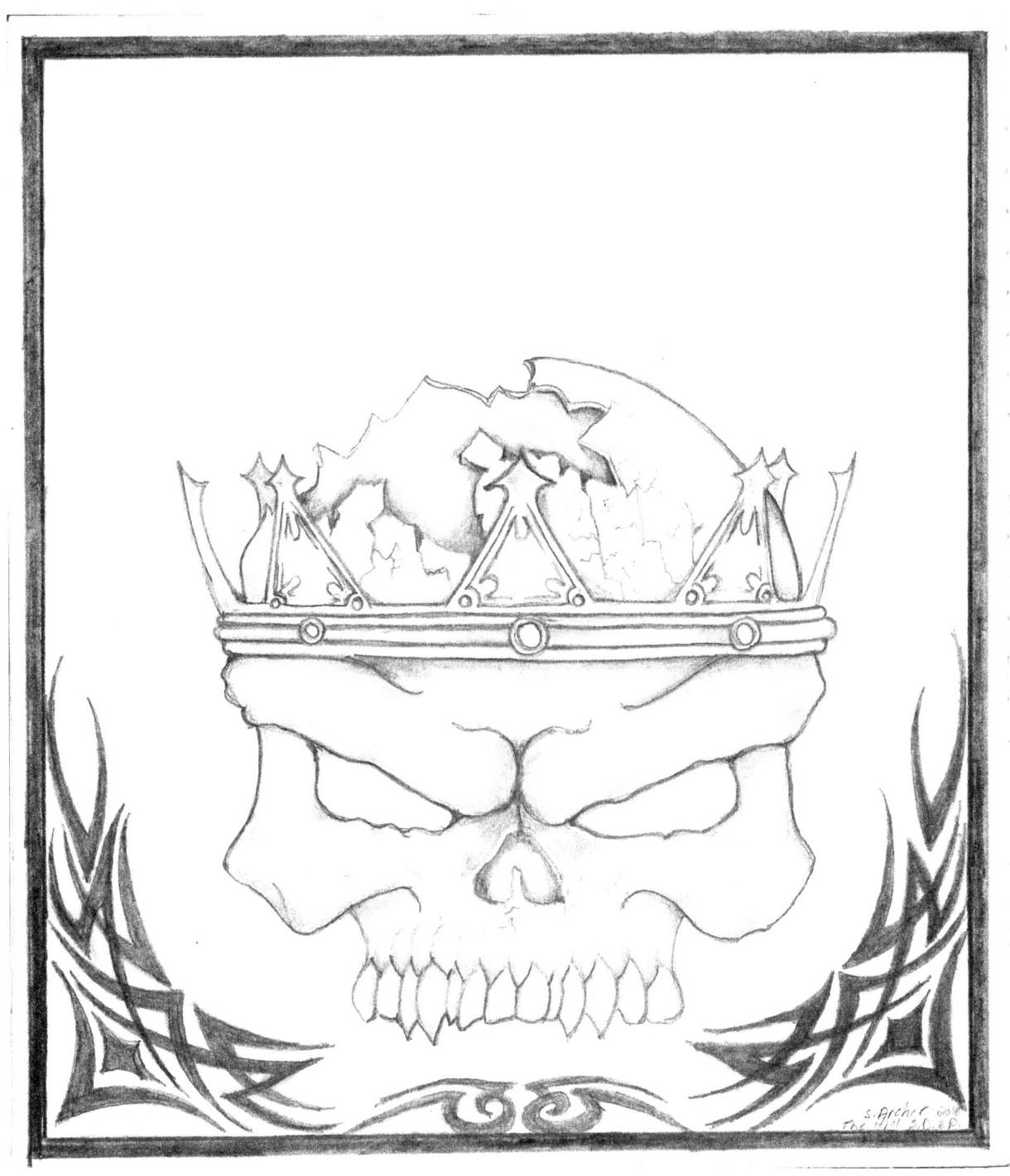

Shane Archer

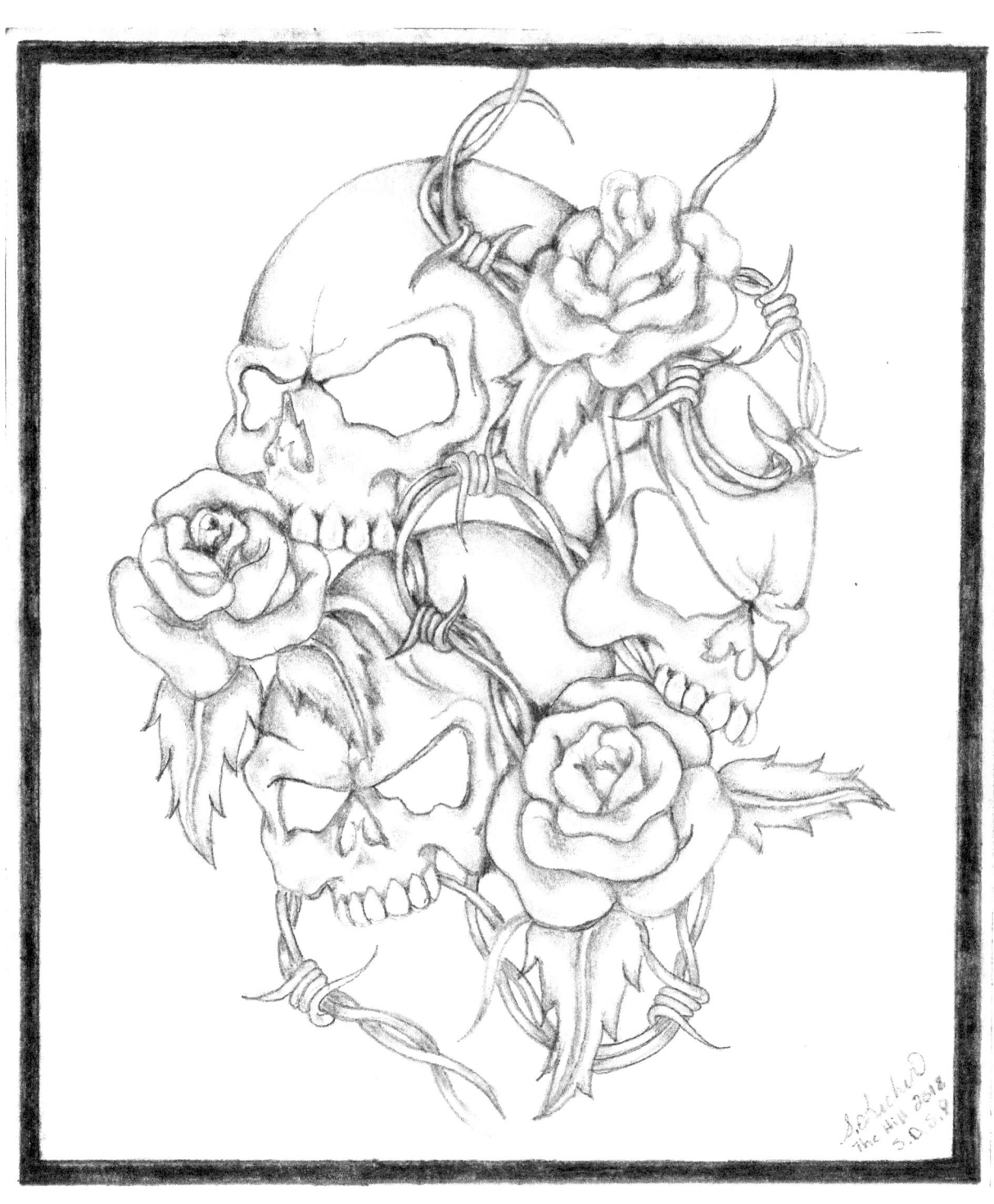

Shane Archer

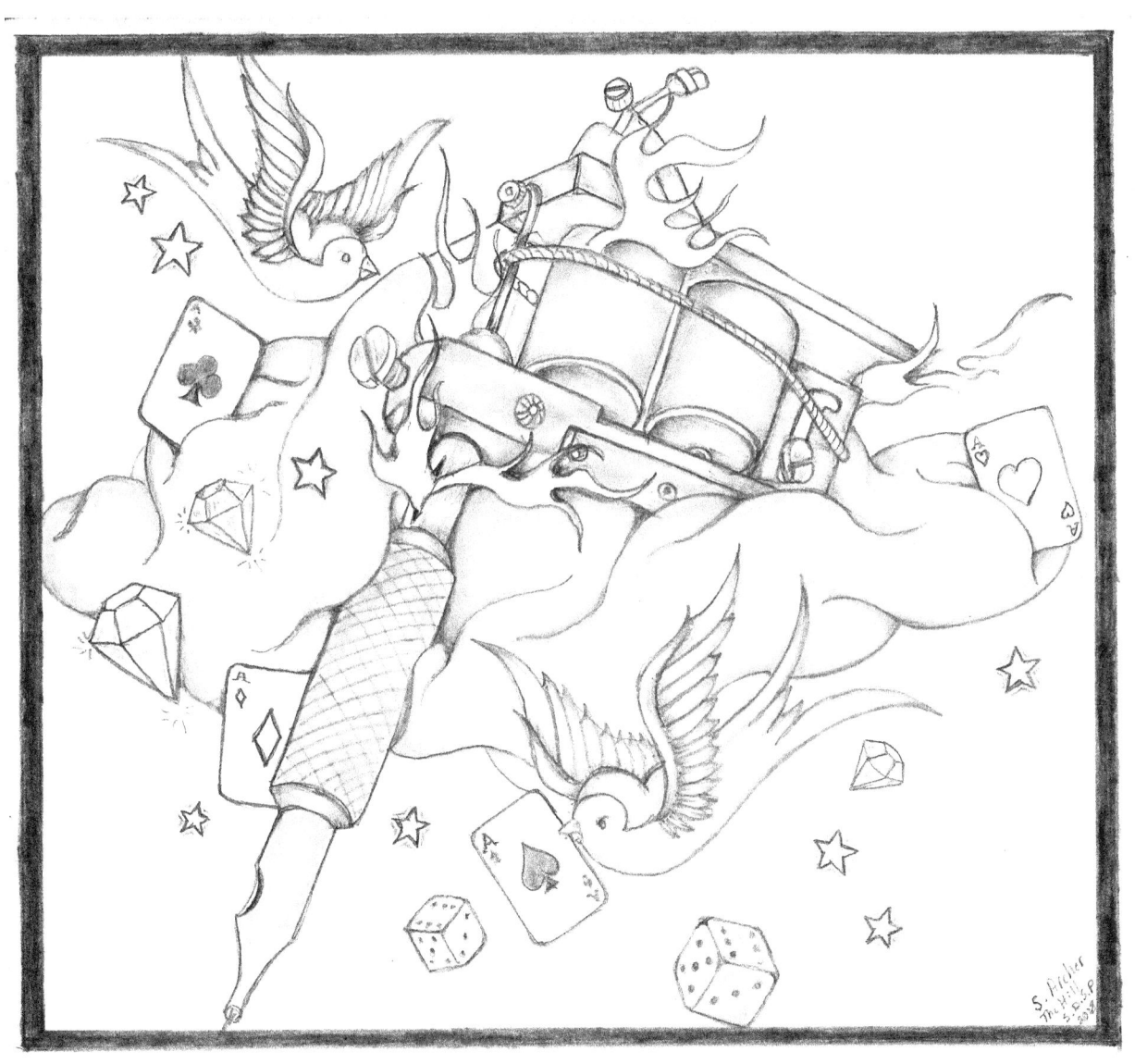

Shane Archer

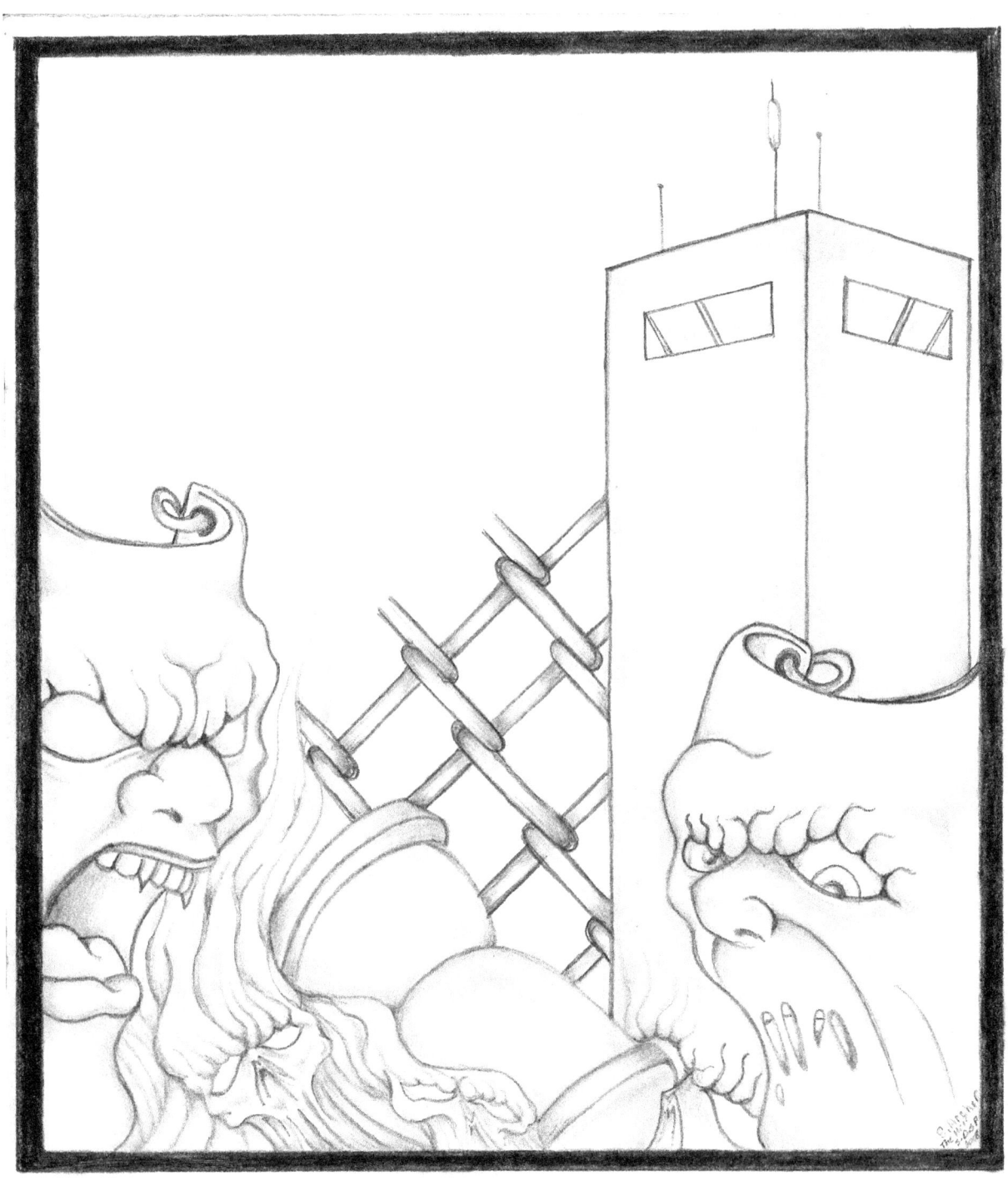

Shane Blake

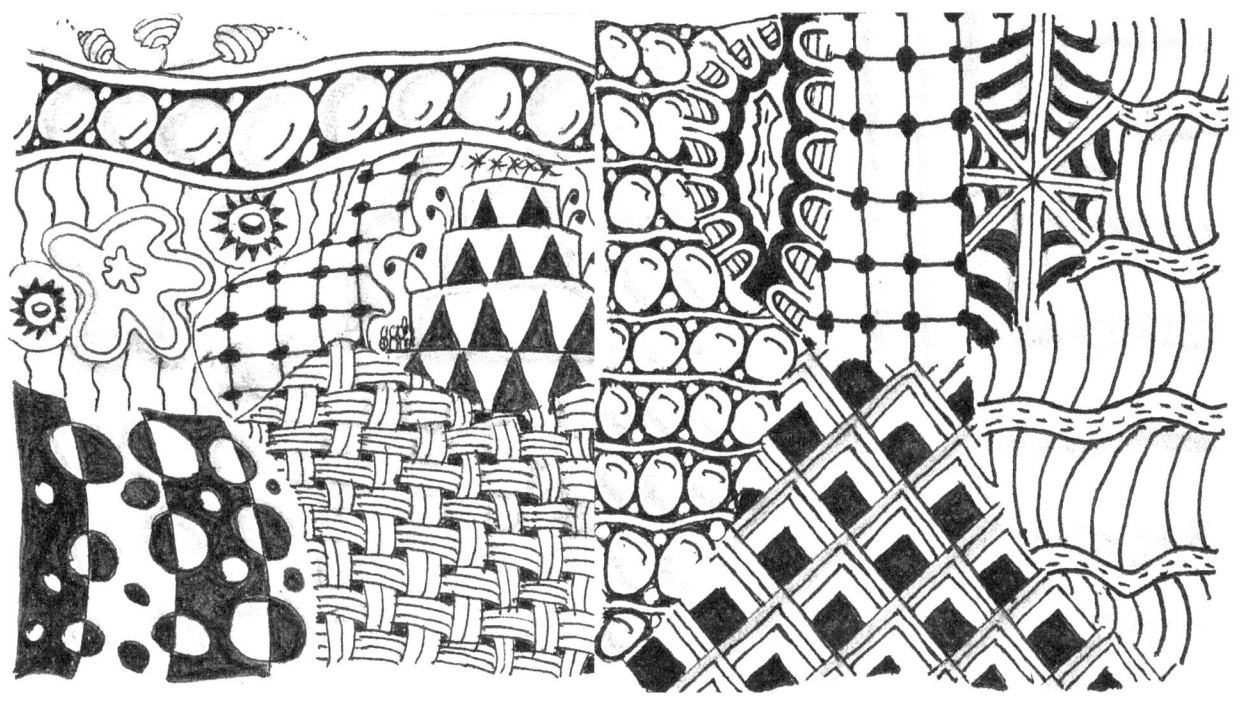

Tyson Hayes

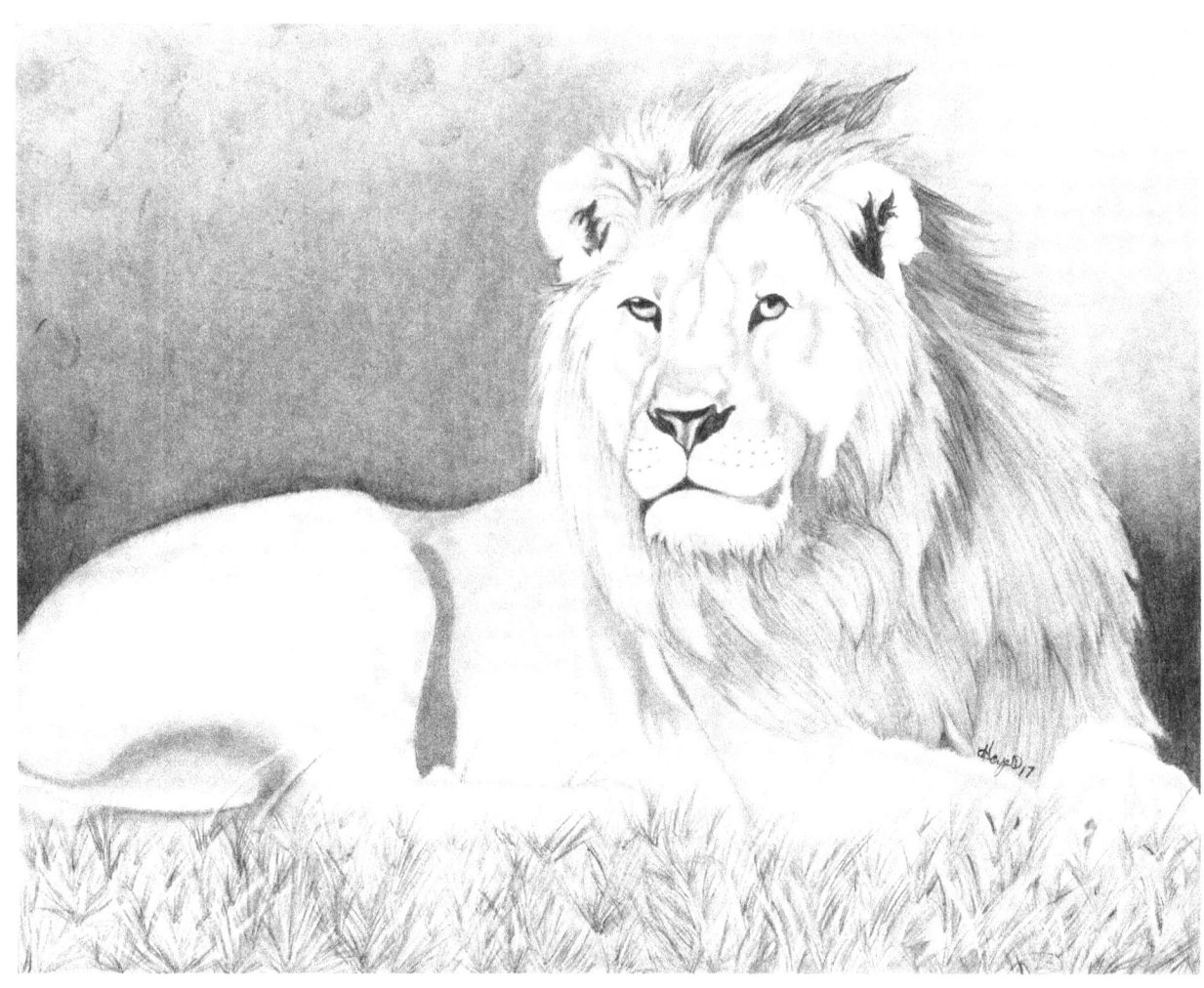

Tyson Hayes

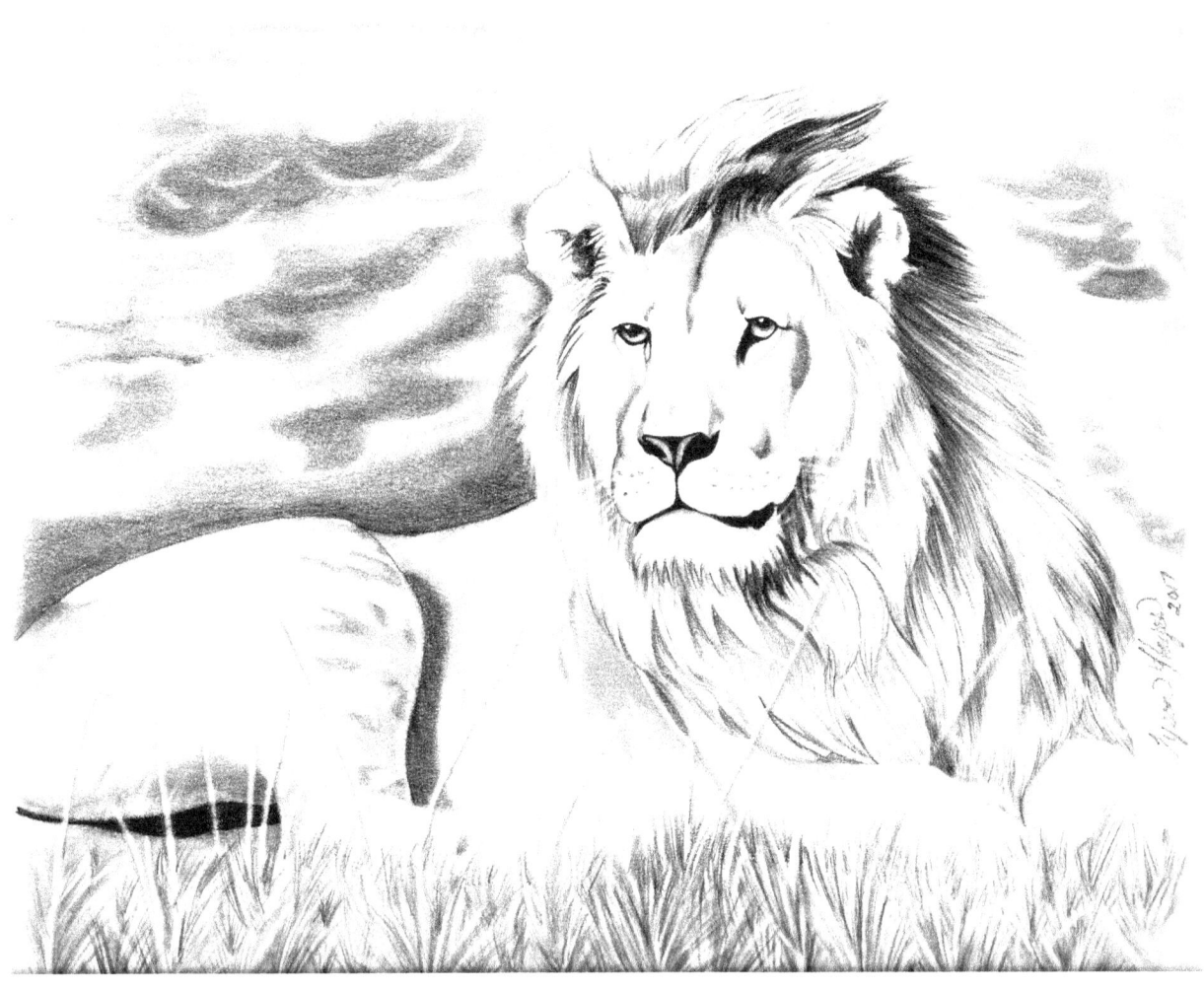

Tyson Hayes

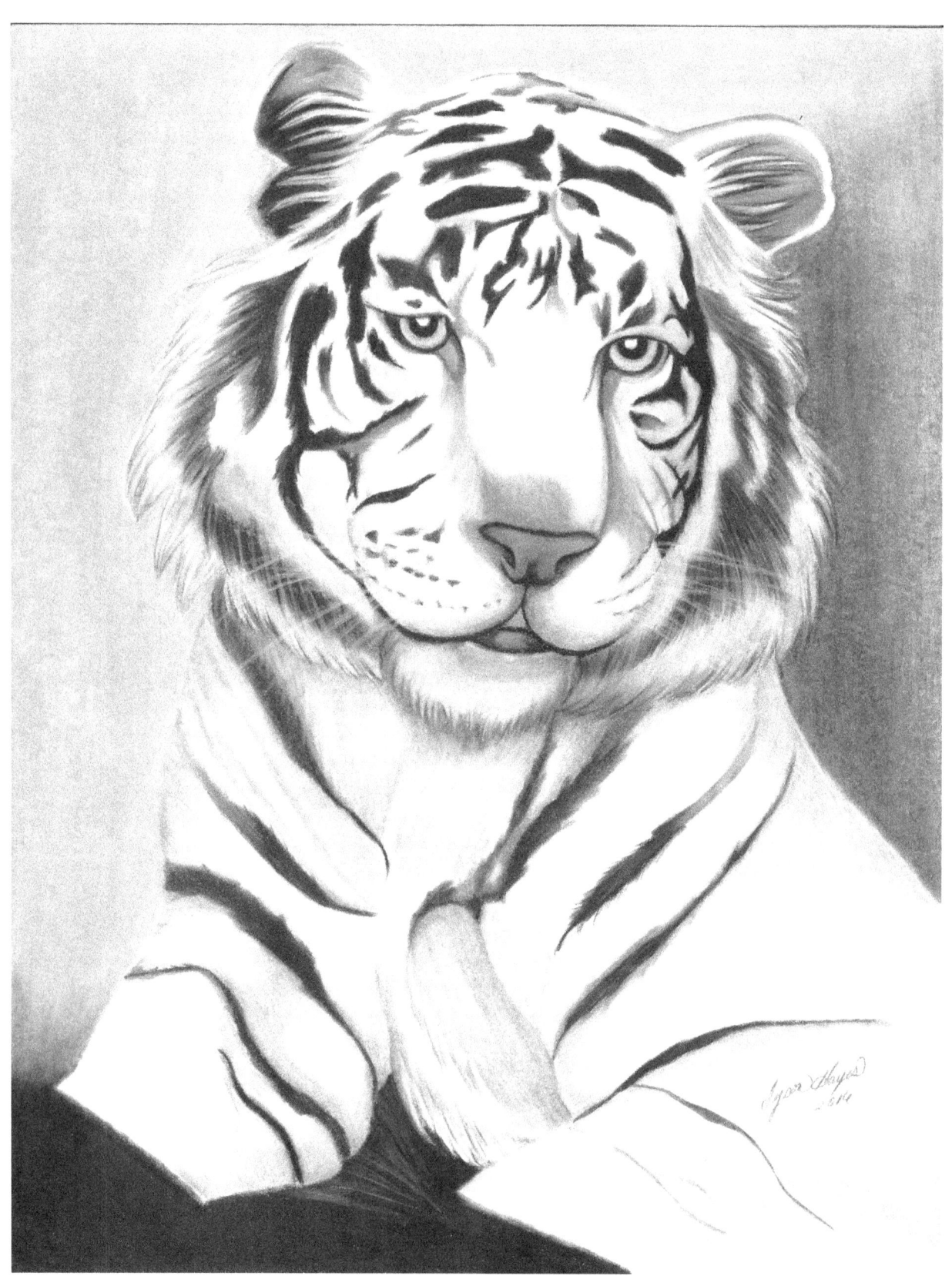

Tyson Hayes

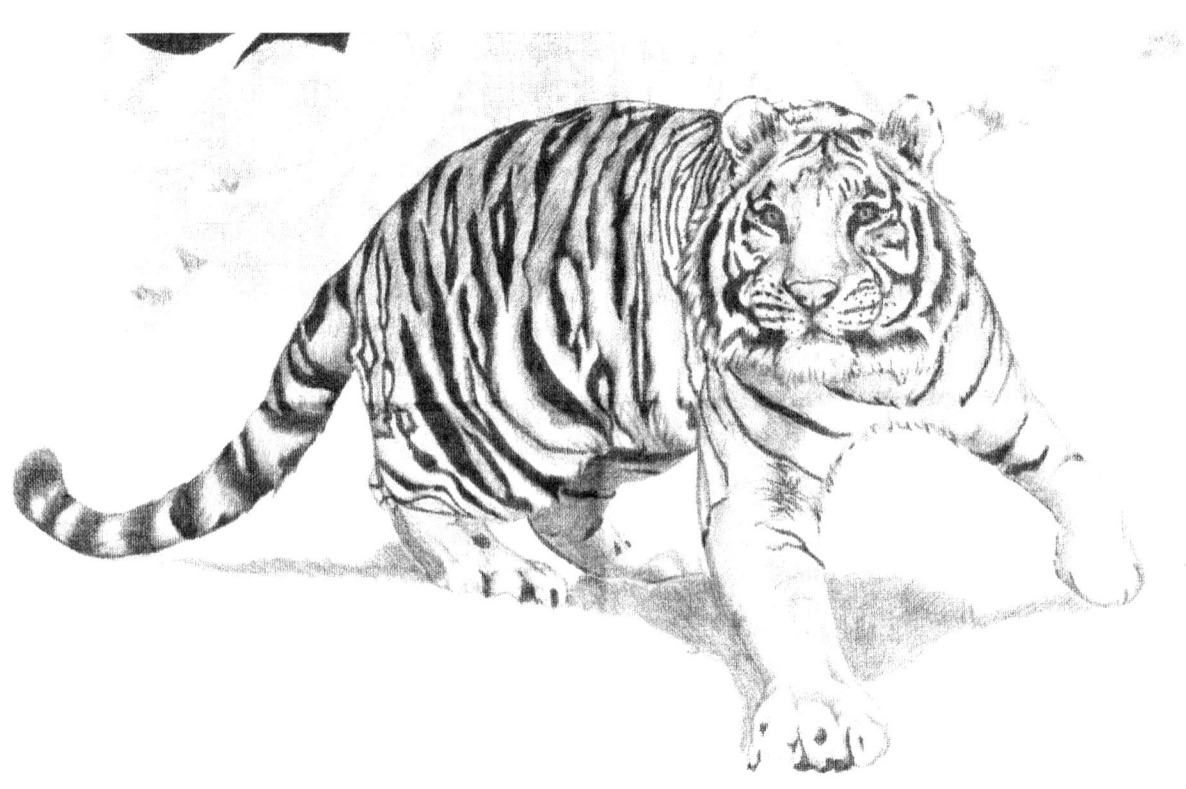

Tyson Hayes

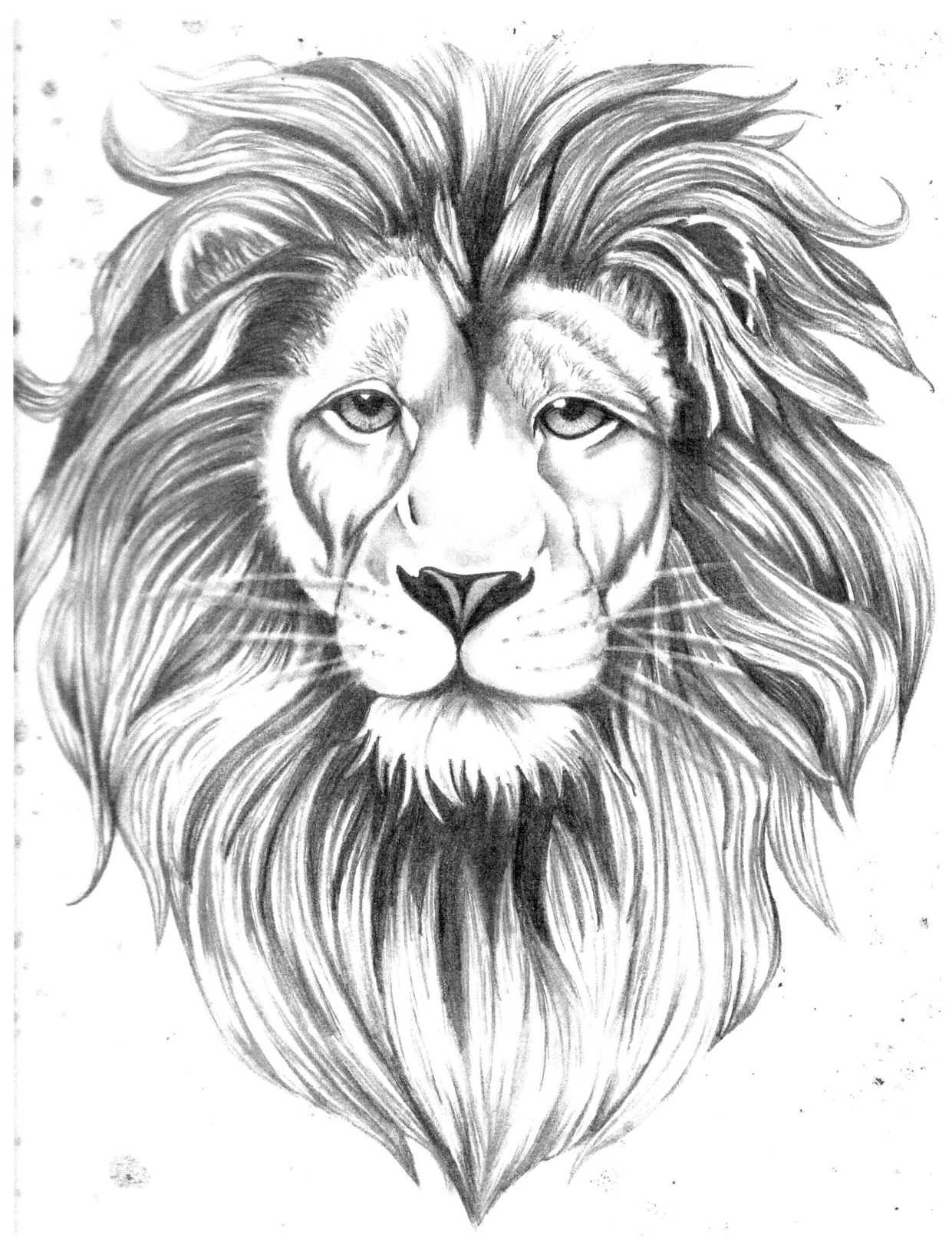

Tyson Hayes

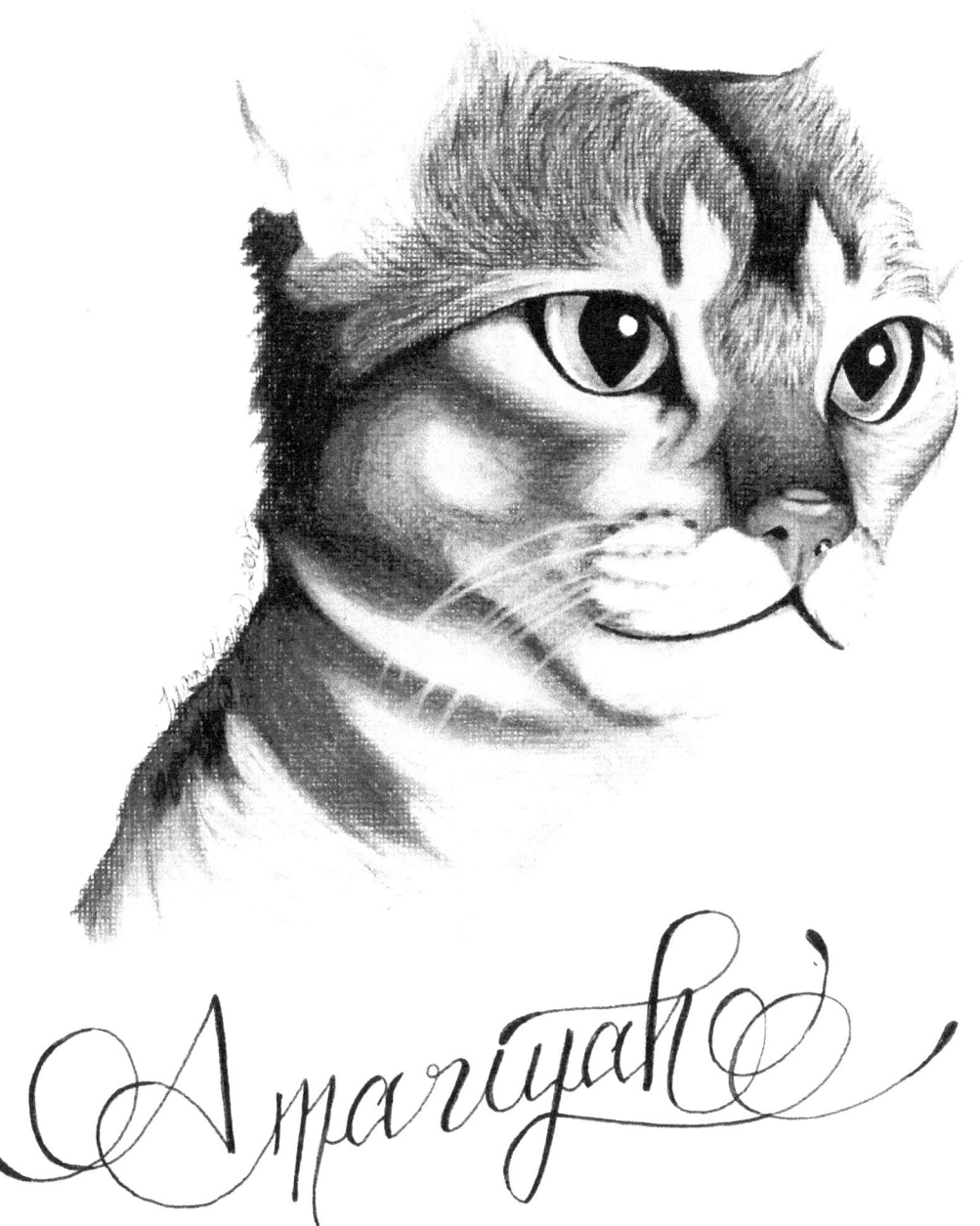

Amariyah

Tyson Hayes

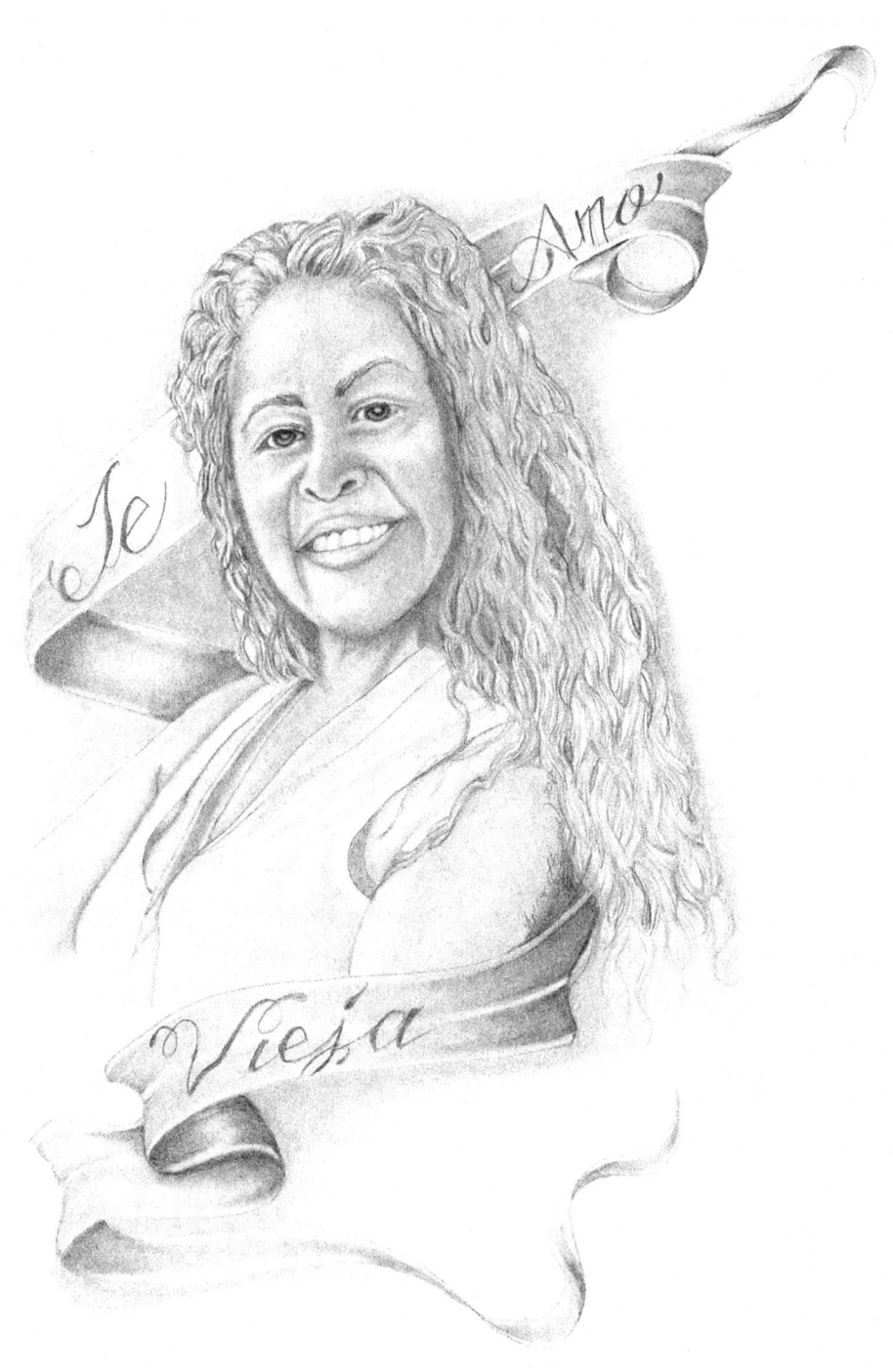

Tyson Hayes

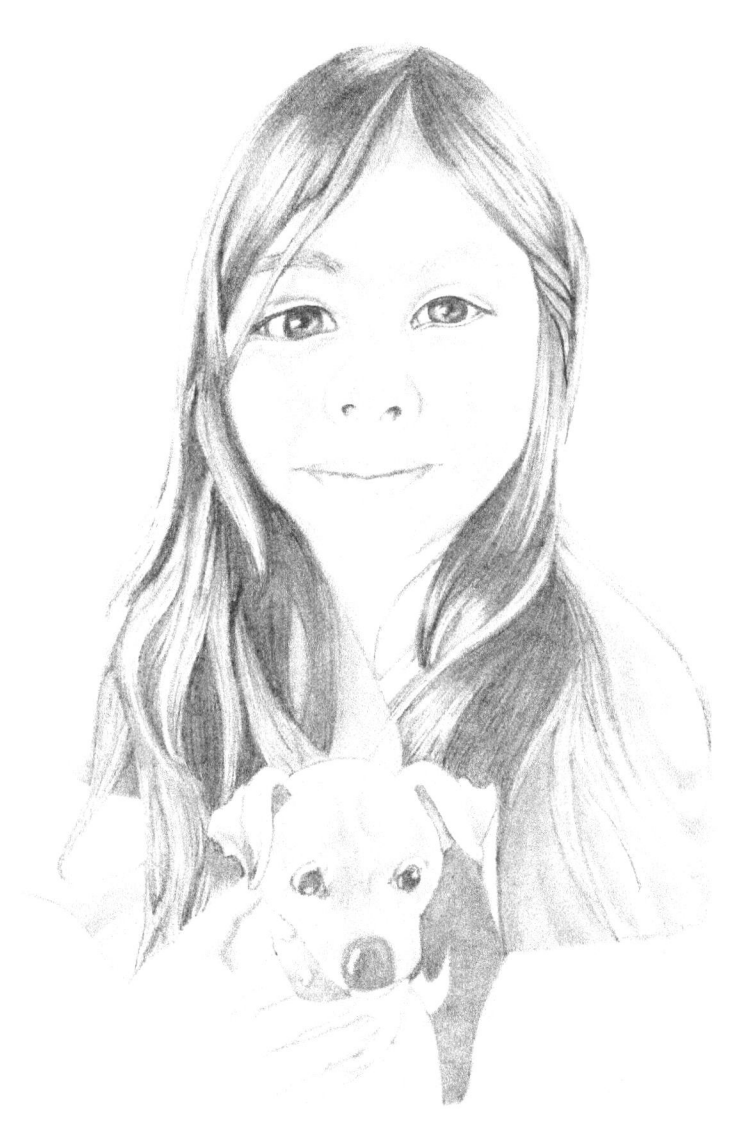

Tyson Hayes

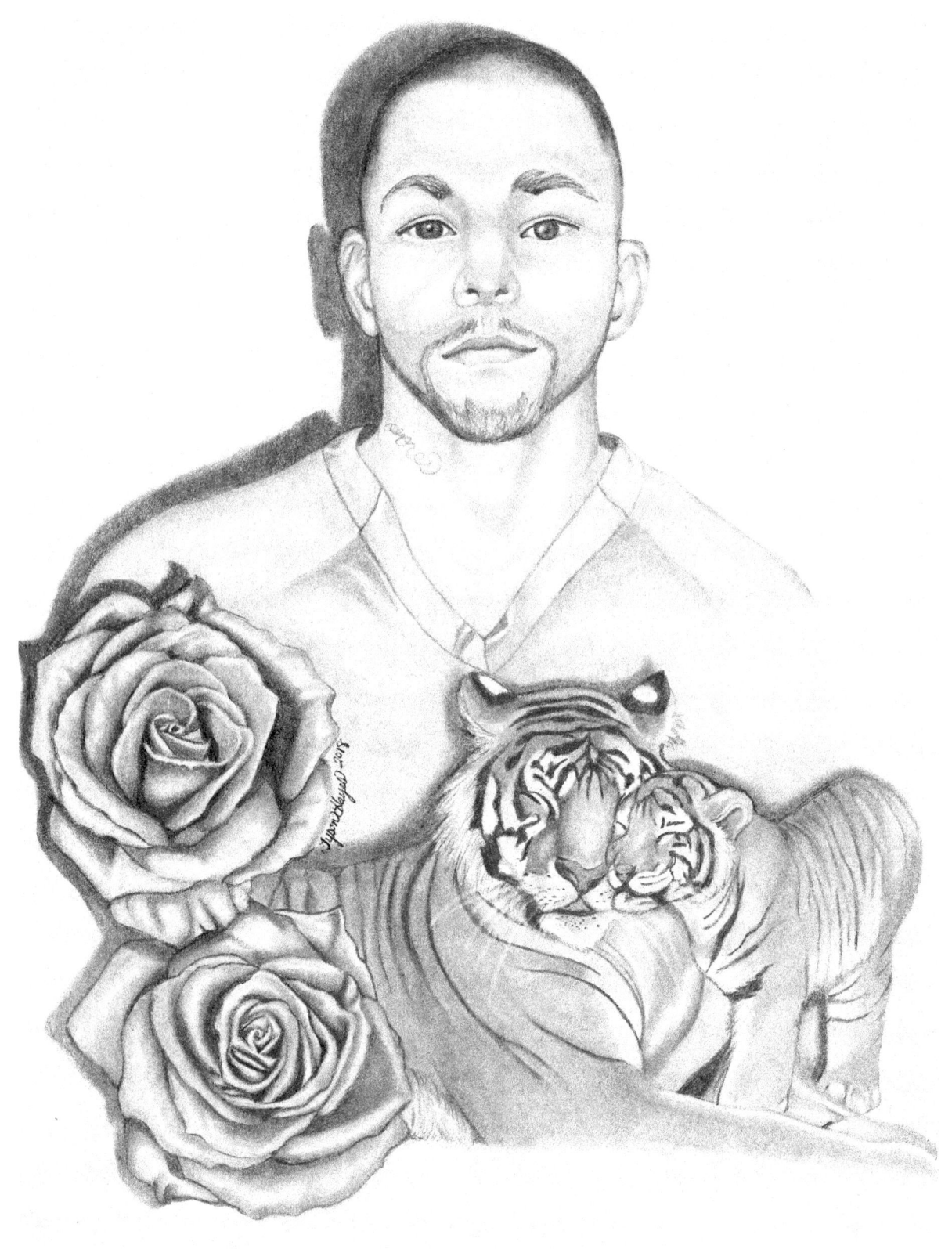

Tyson Hayes

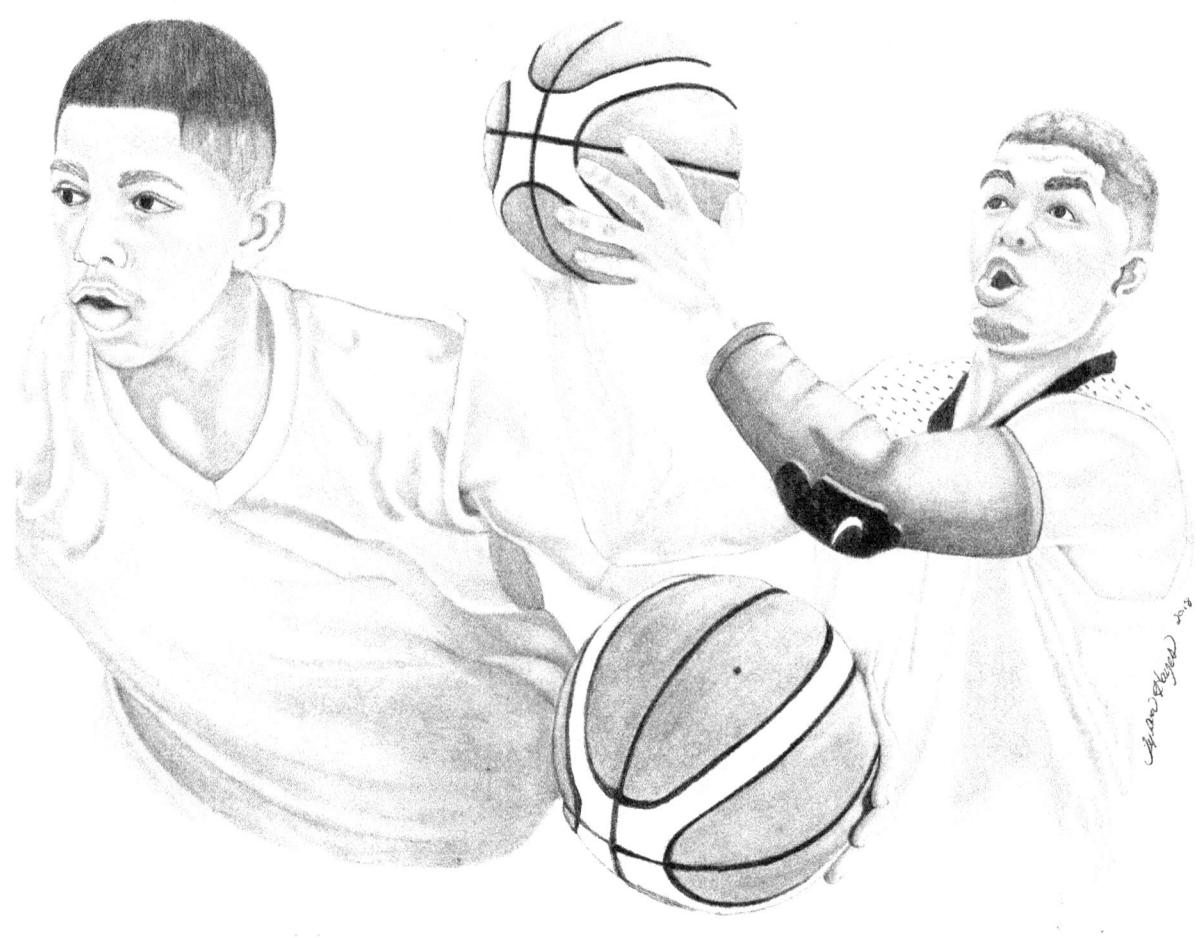

Tyson Hayes

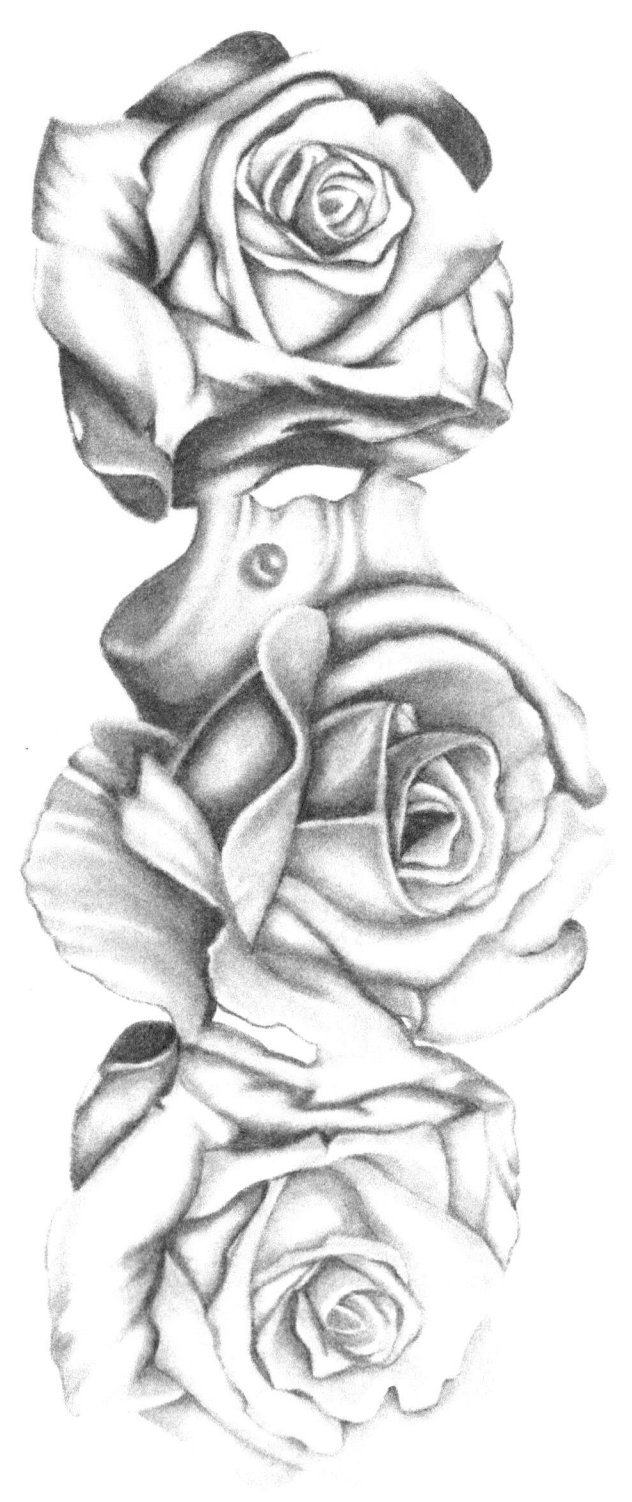

Tyson Hayes

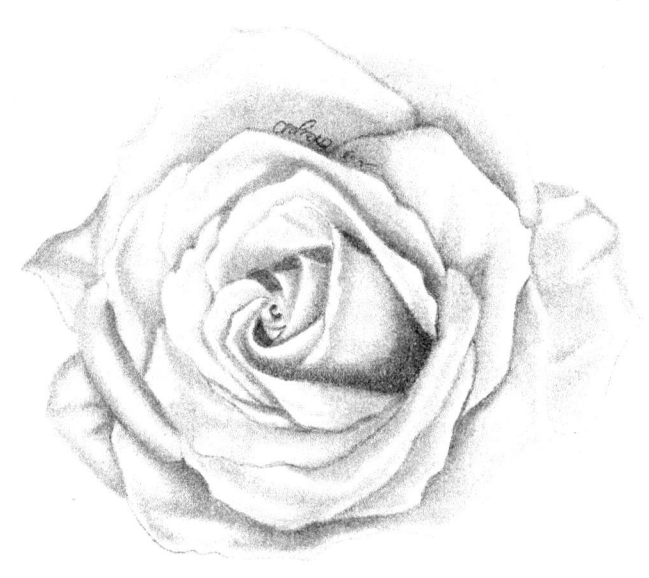

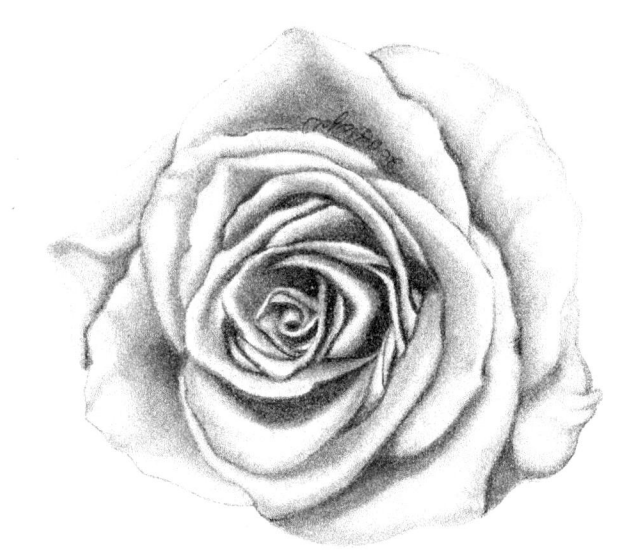

Tyson Hayes

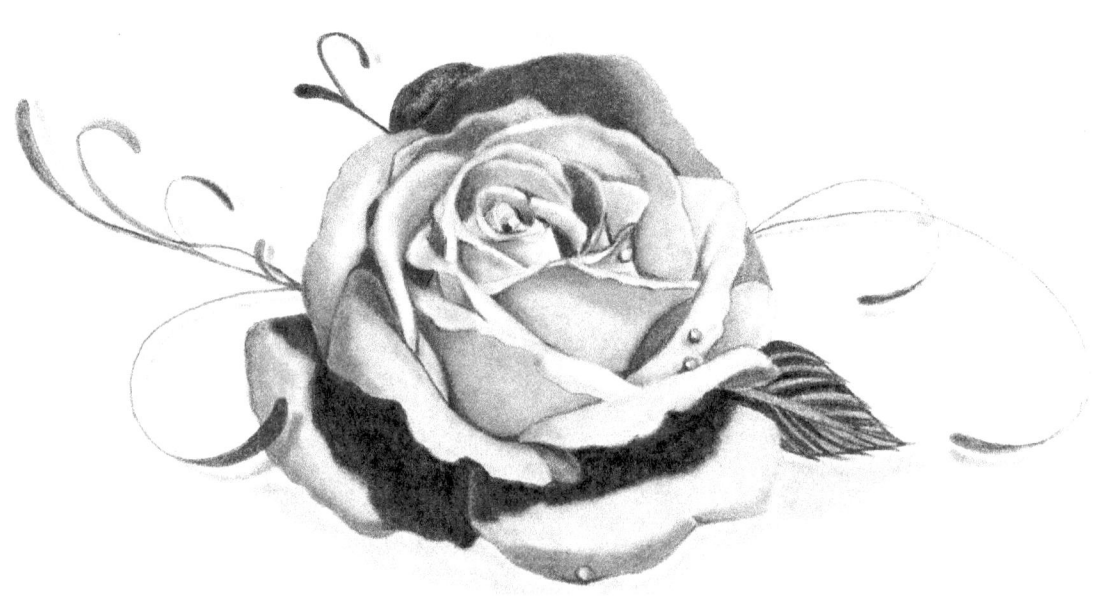

Tyson Hayes

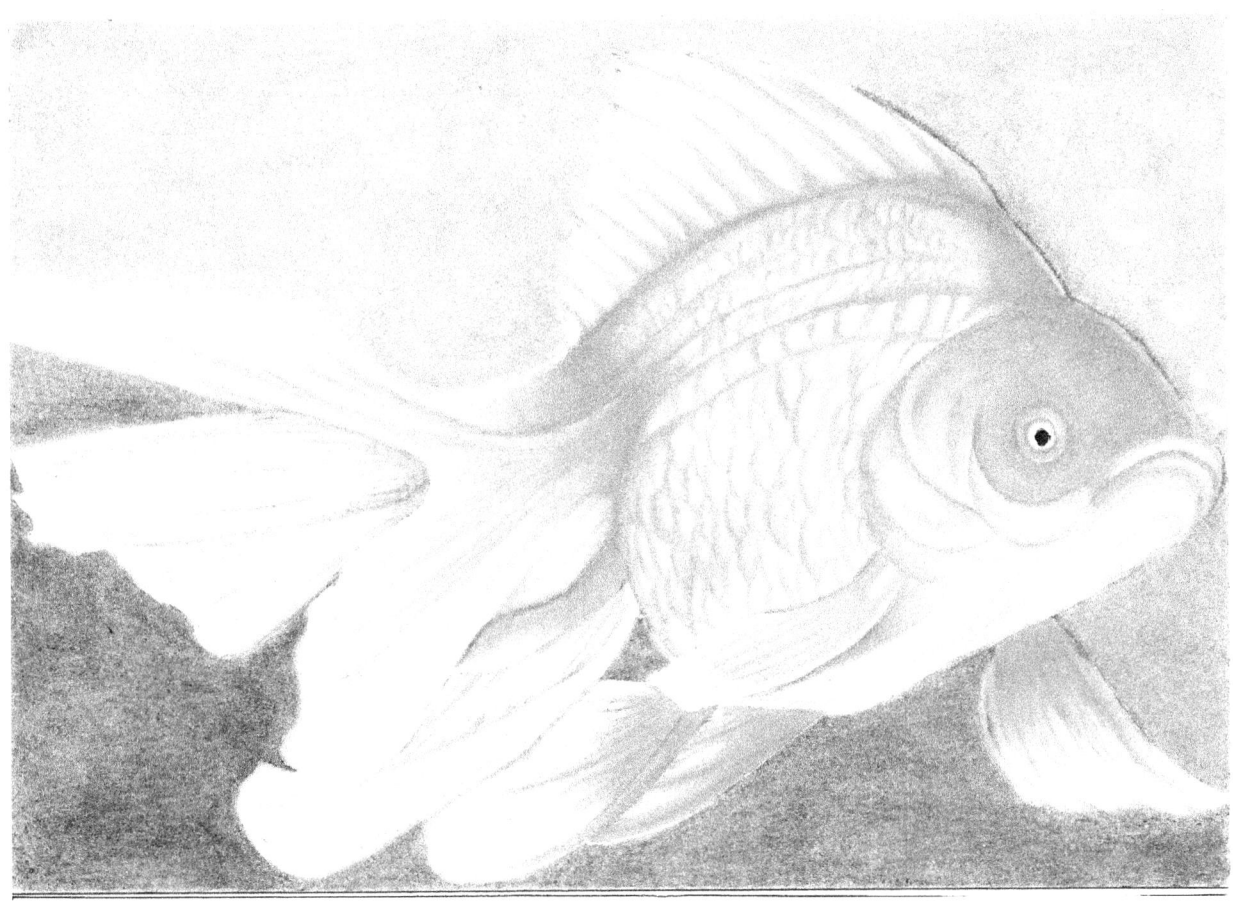

Tyson Hayes

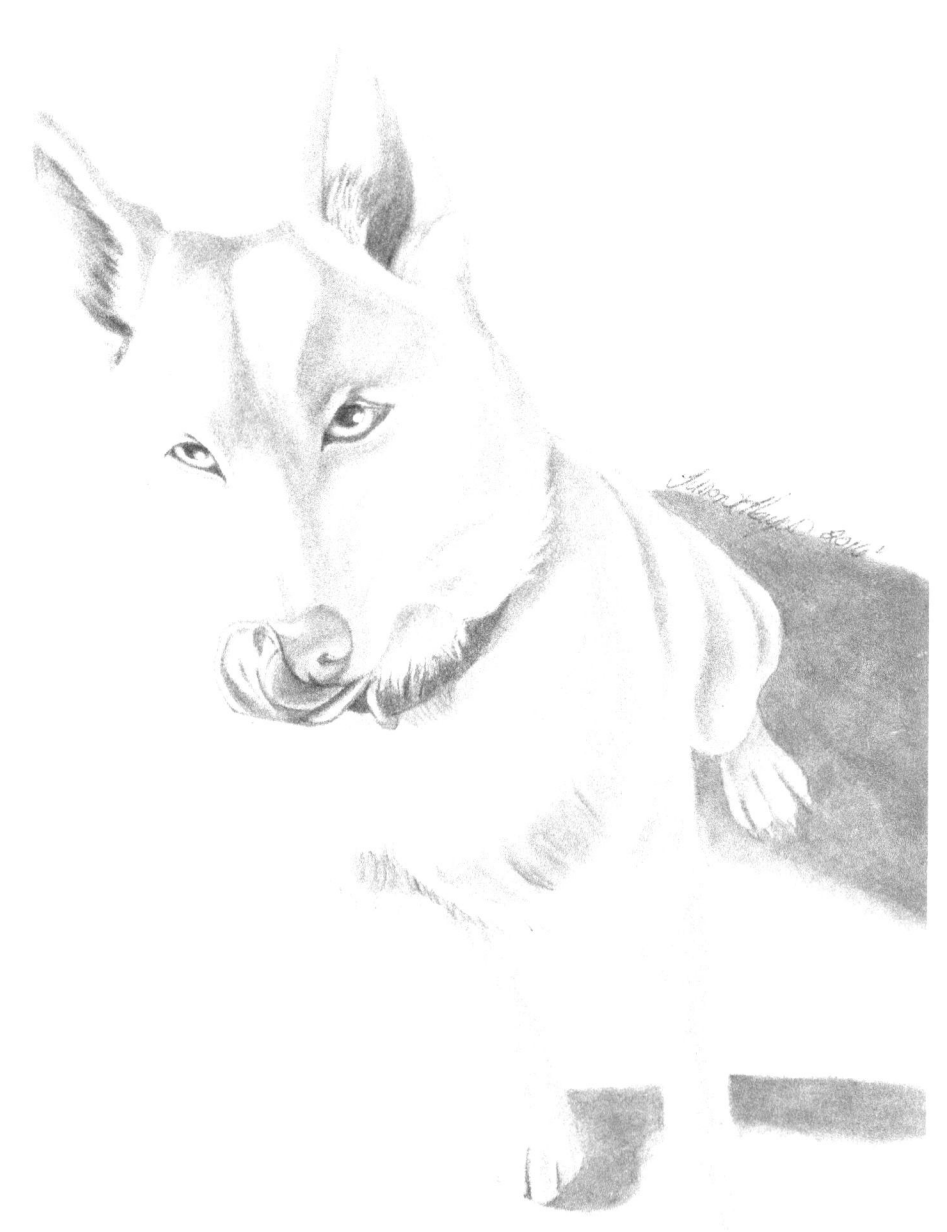

Tyson Hayes

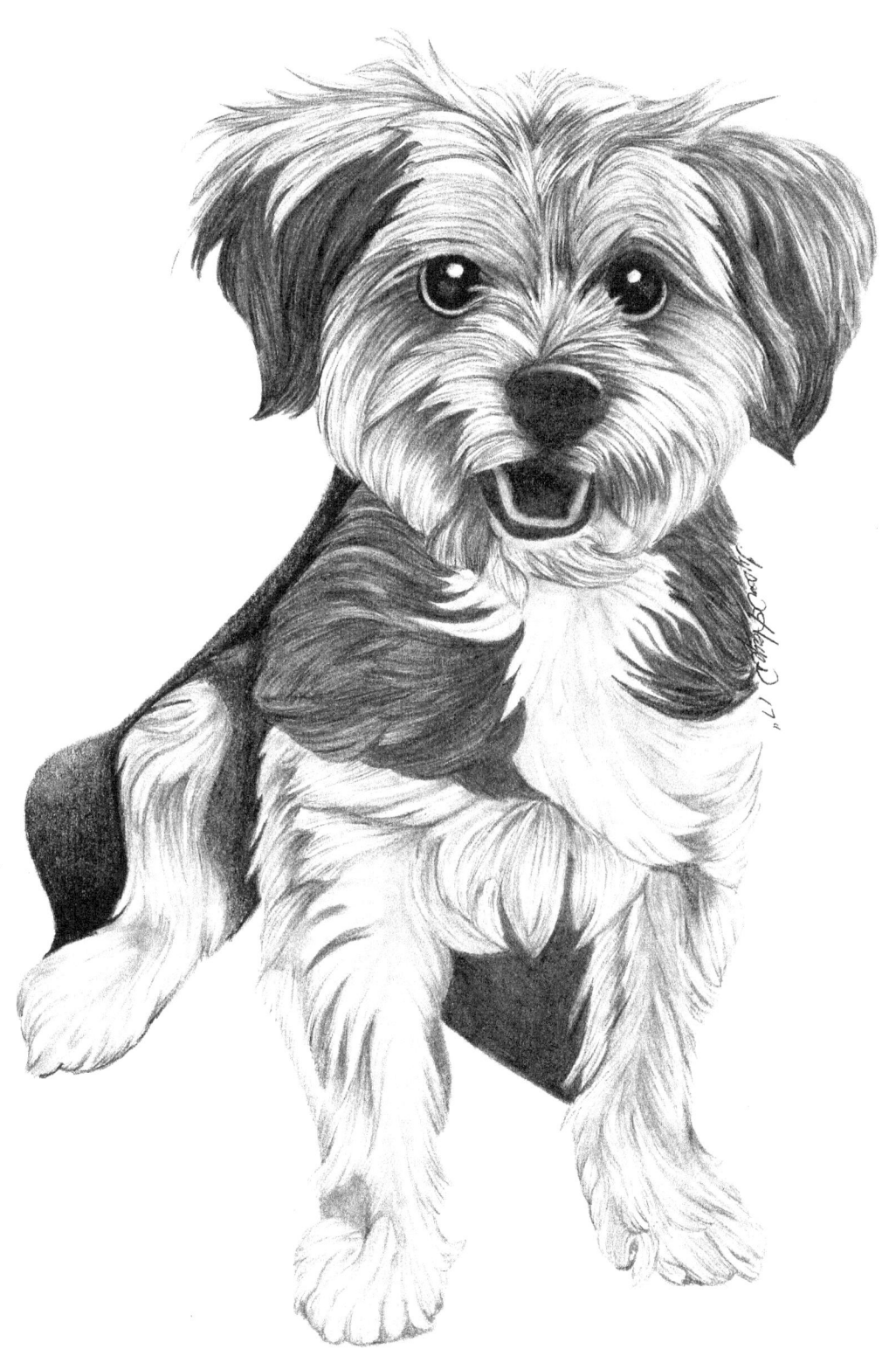

Tyson Hayes

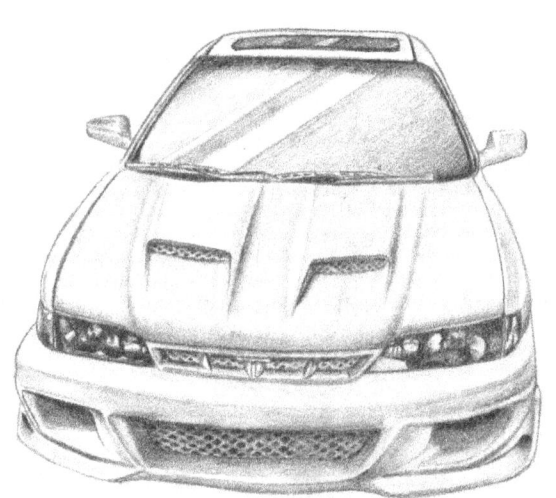

Tyson Hayes

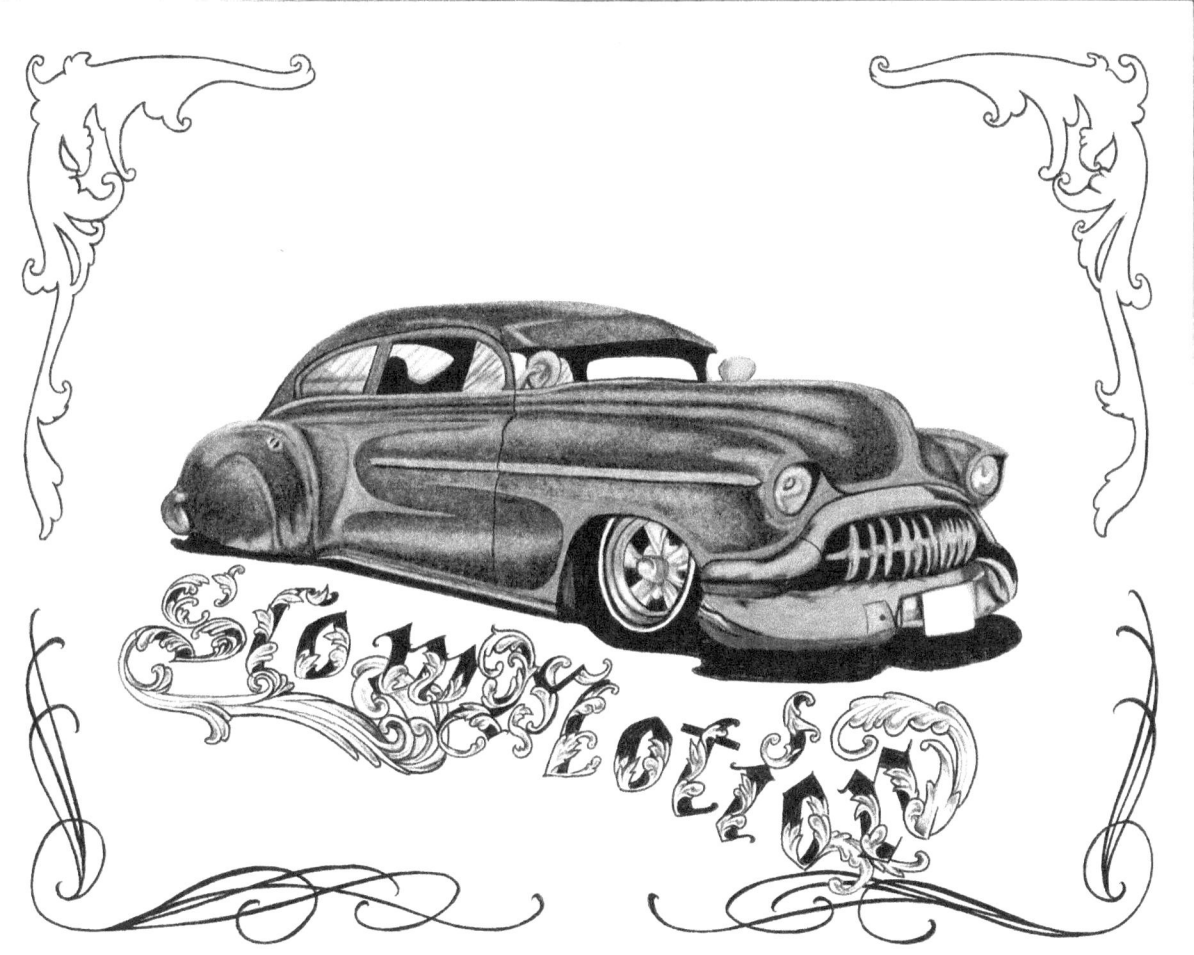

Tyson Hayes

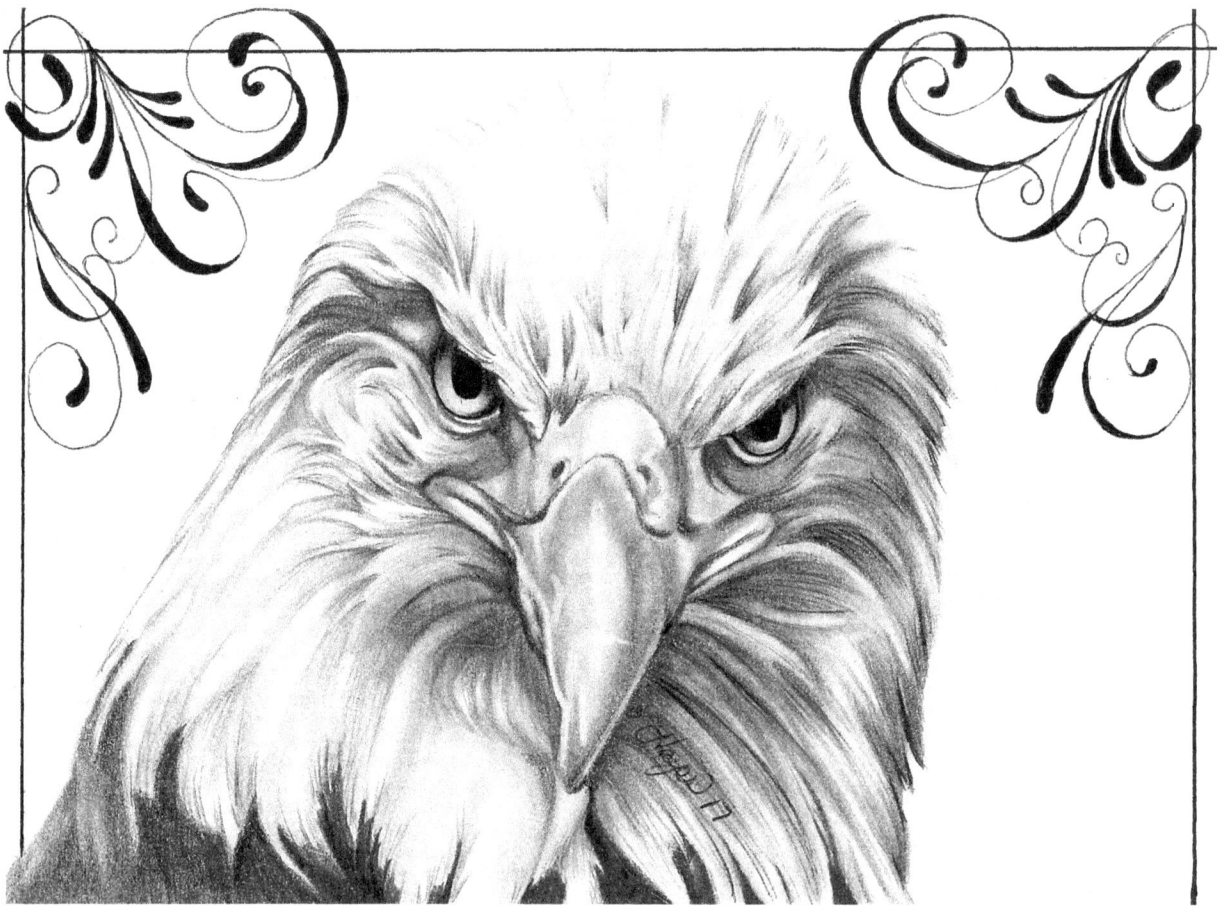

Tyson Hayes

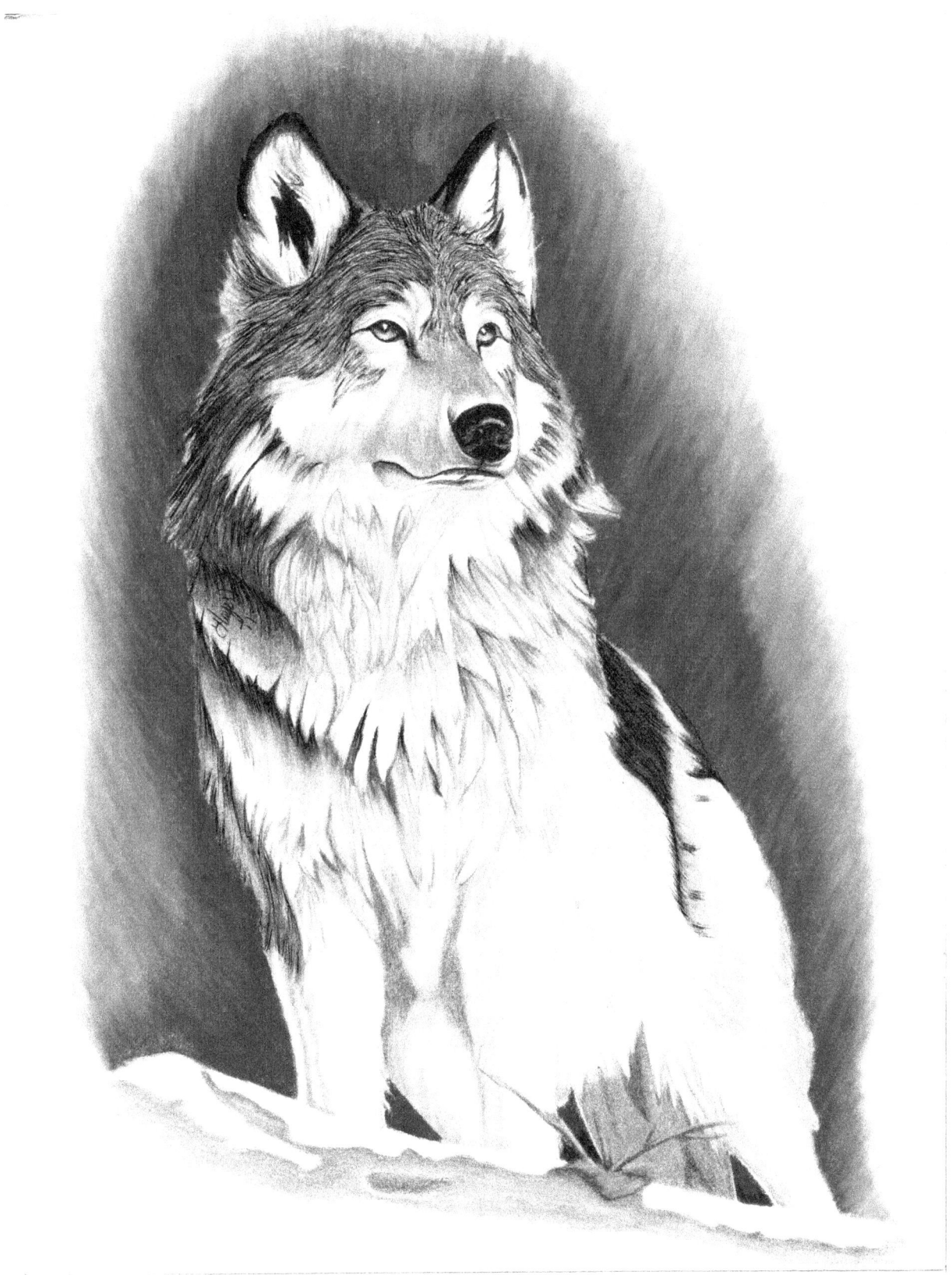

Tyson Hayes

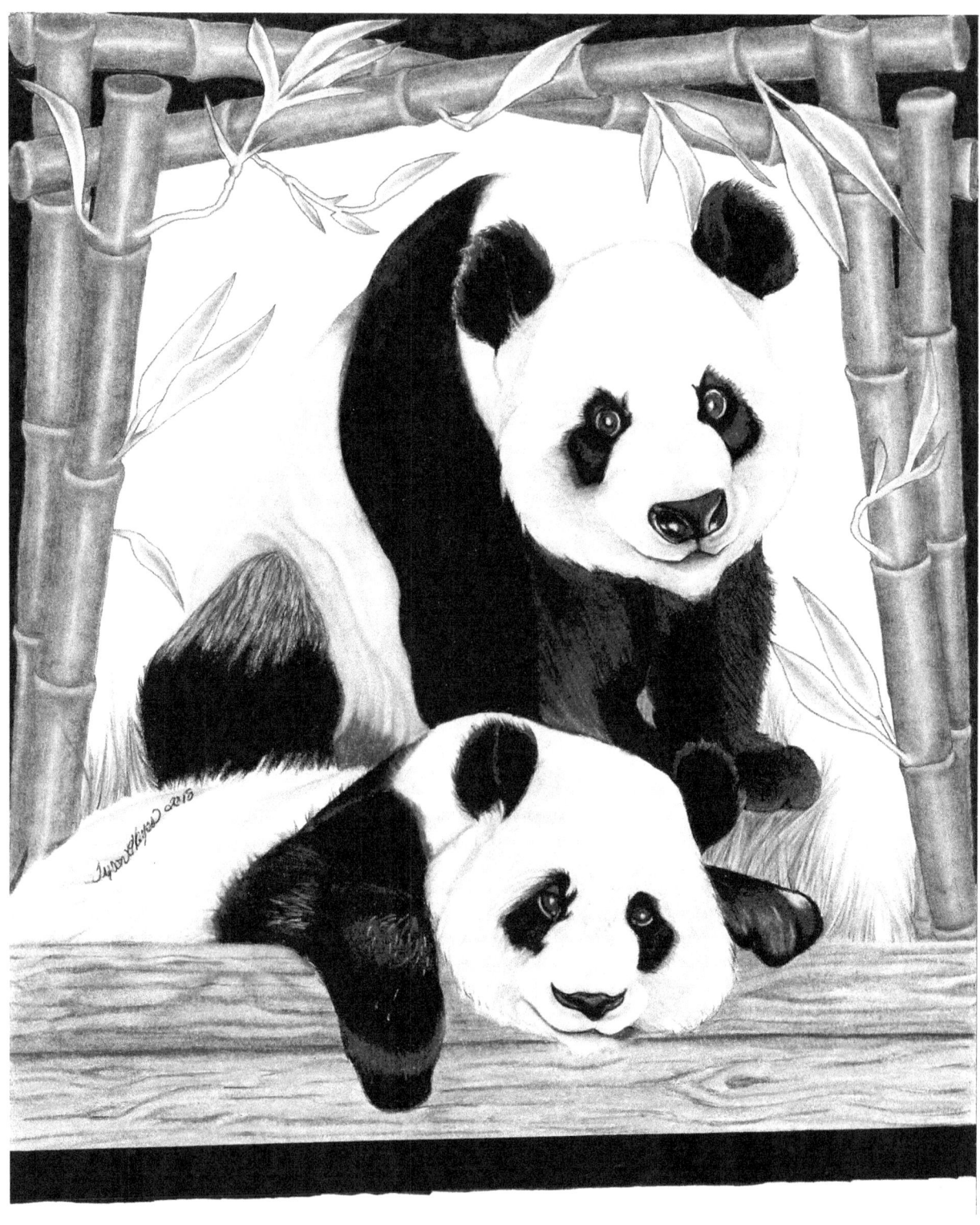

Tyson Hayes

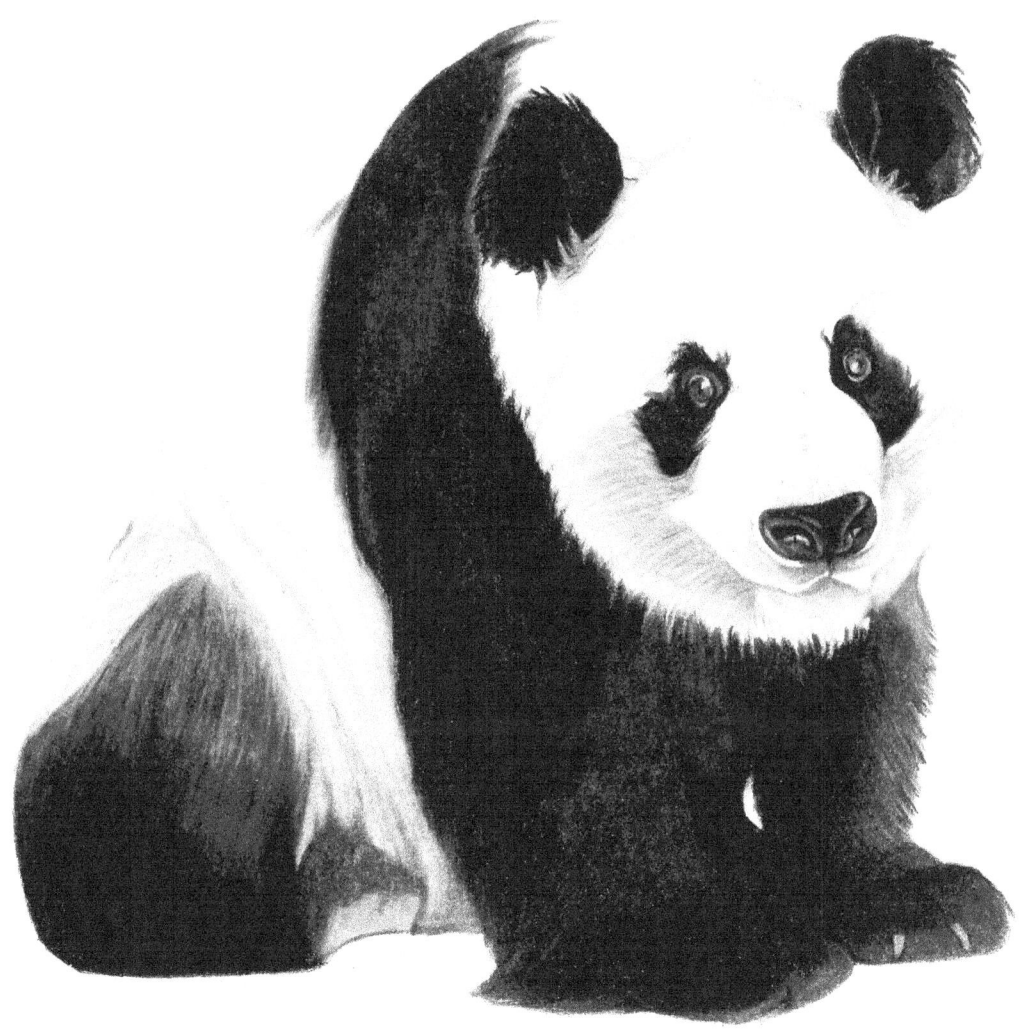

Tyson Hayes

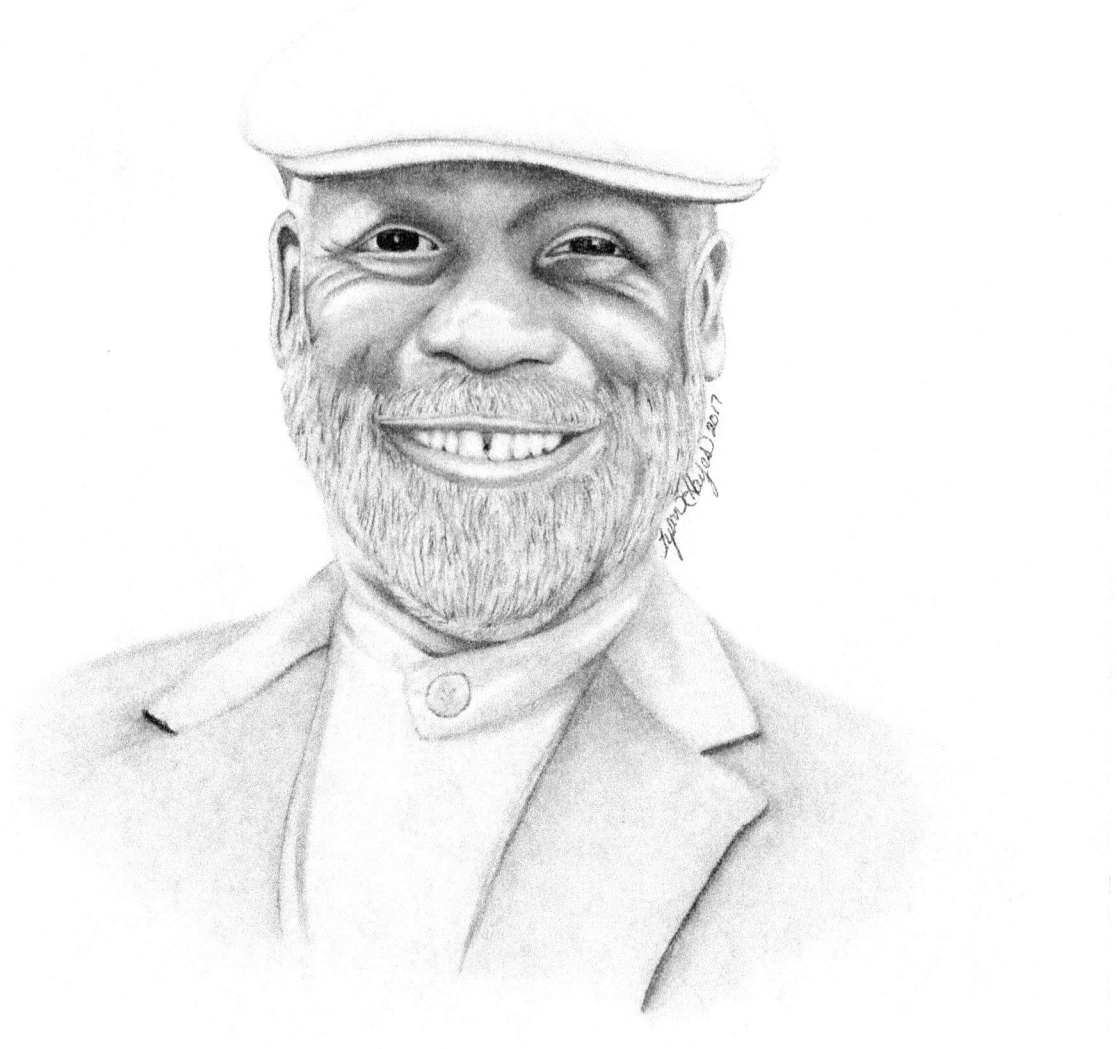

Tyson Hayes

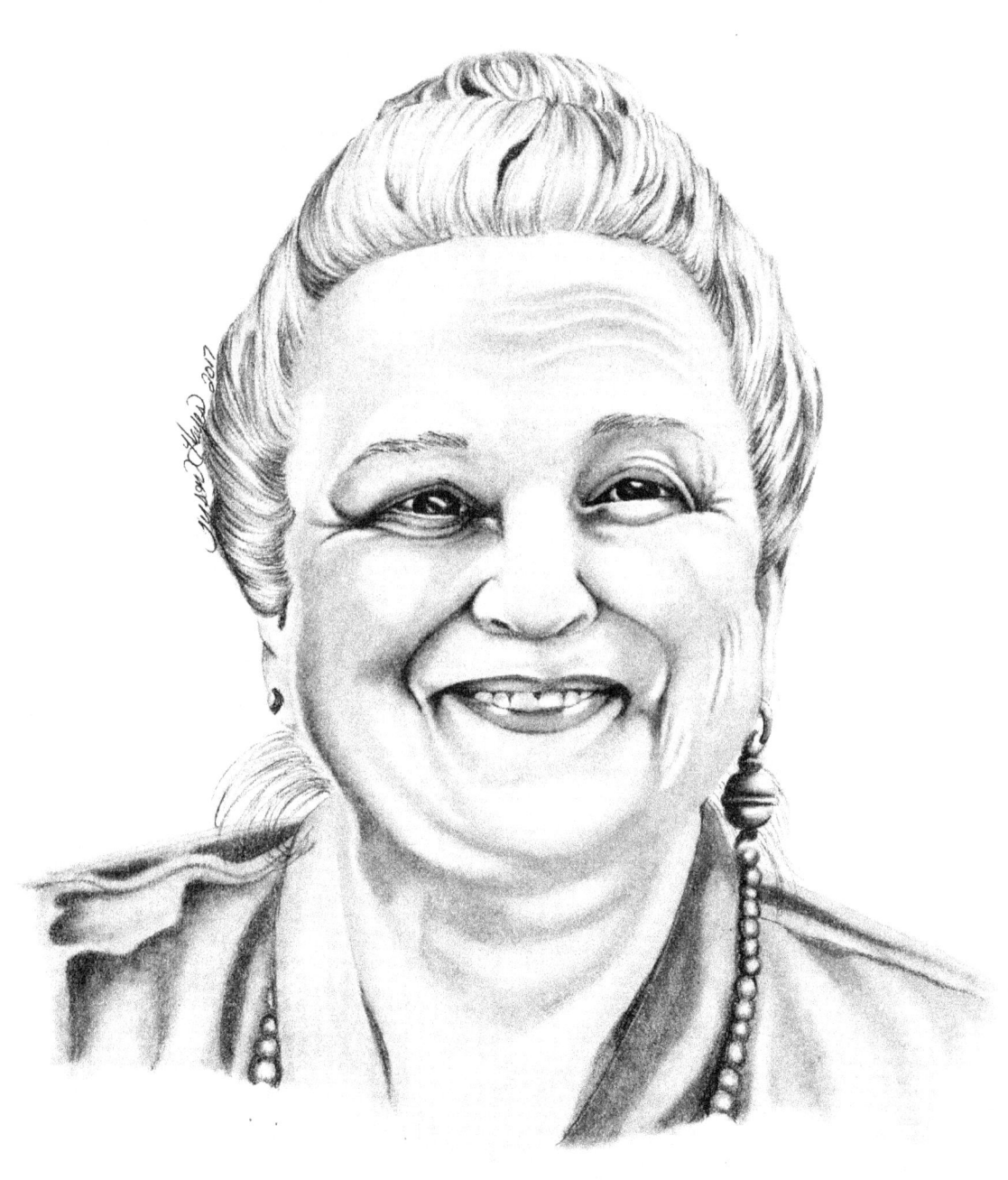

Tyson Hayes

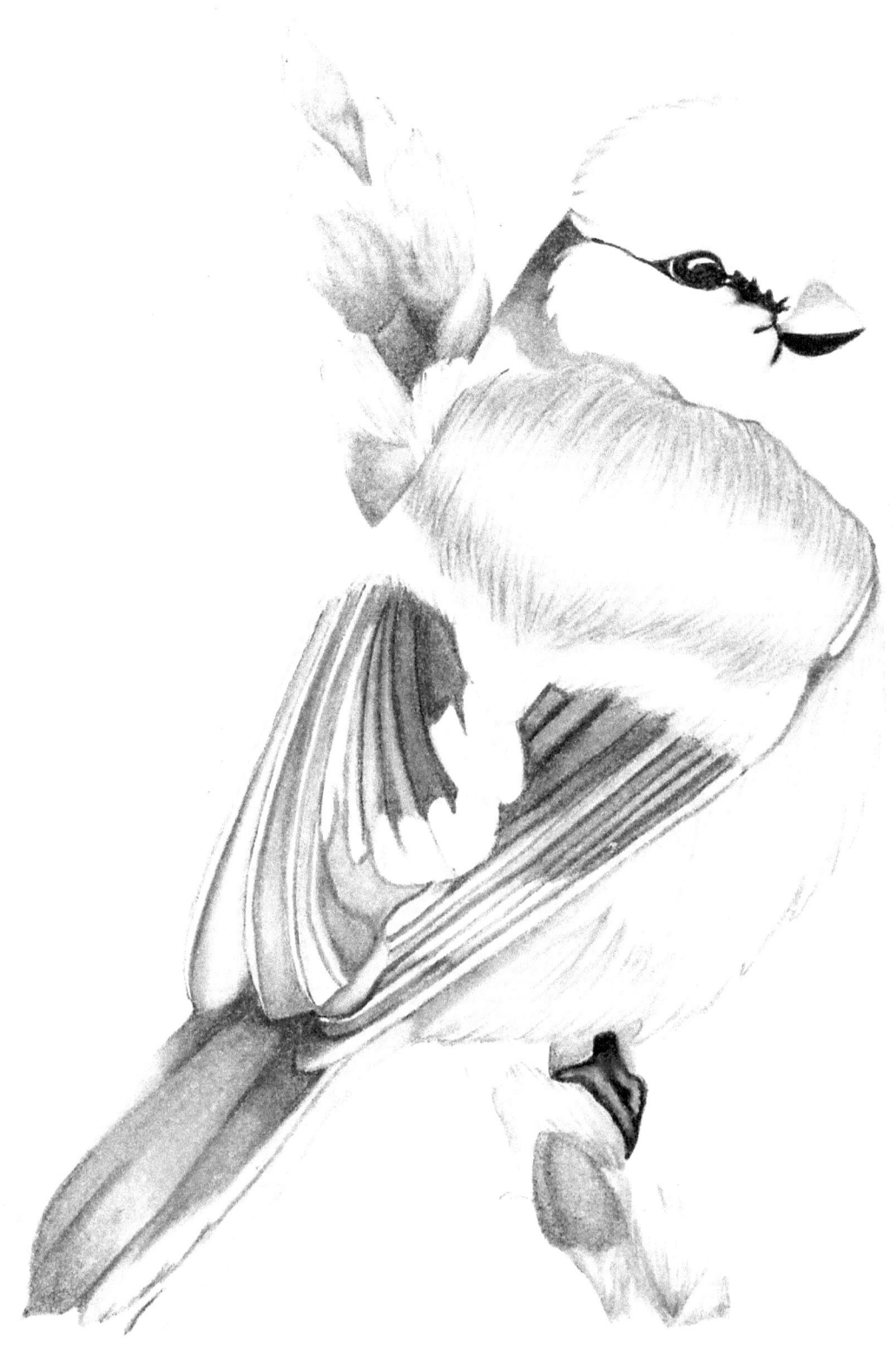